A GARDENER'S GUIDE TO
BOX

Designing, shaping and caring for *Buxus*

A GARDENER'S GUIDE TO

BOX

Designing, shaping and caring for *Buxus*

JENNY ALBAN DAVIES

THE CROWOOD PRESS

First published in 2022 by
The Crowood Press Ltd
Ramsbury, Marlborough
Wiltshire SN8 2HR

enquiries@crowood.com

www.crowood.com

British Library Cataloguing-in-Publication Data
A catalogue record for this book is available from the British Library.

ISBN 978 0 7198 4075 3

Cover
Troutbeck, Kent

Frontispiece
Helmingham Hall, Suffolk

Typeset and designed by D & N Publishing, Baydon, Wiltshire
Cover design by Blue Sunflower Creative
Printed and bound in India by Parksons Graphics

CONTENTS

ACKNOWLEDGEMENTS

My husband Huw, who has been my mainstay, has contributed so much in the writing of my manuscript. To him I most affectionately dedicate this book.

I am extremely grateful to Lynn Batdorf, previously curator of the National Boxwood Collection, United States National Arboretum, Washington, DC, for his valuable advice and the genuine interest he has taken in my book. His expertise in matters relating to box is unequalled, as is his generosity in spending time and sharing his knowledge with other enthusiasts. The chapters on box species and cultivars, and pests and diseases benefited in particular from his help. Chris Poole of the European Boxwood and Topiary Society (EBTS) has also given enormous assistance, as well as making suggestions and providing images. The EBTS is a powerhouse for everyone with an interest in box and topiary and it gives its members up-to-date information and practical support. Anne Jennings was extremely helpful and I am grateful to her for sharing her considerable experience. A special word of thanks to my family for their encouragement and help throughout.

Picture Acknowledgements

During the course of writing the book I visited a number of houses and gardens with outstanding displays of box, which are featured in the book. The owners of Restoration House, Jonathan Wilmot and Robert Tucker, were very kind to allow me to visit and photograph the annual clipping of the outstanding parterre in 2021 and I am indebted to the gardeners, Aaron Danton and Tim Schooley for their cooperation. The display of box at Old Place Farm is inspirational and I am very grateful to Jeffrey Eker for allowing me to photograph the garden, which is a celebration of the creativity of his wife, Ann. I am also grateful to Sigi Aiken for allowing me to photograph her beautiful garden at Horns Lodge.

A number of people have been very kind in sending me photographs, or allowing me to take photographs of their gardens. Without their enthusiastic help my book would have been very poorly populated with images and I am indebted to them all:

Sarah Jones, Celia Dickinson, Kate Howie, John Edge, Vanessa Welsh, Lizzie Bradley, Peter Clark Tree and Garden Services, Max Davies, Chris Poole, Christopher Goode, Gail Jenner, Marie Jessel, Nicki Talbot, Sue Dancey Design, Diane Baistow, Barry Clarke, the owners of Hill Farm Monmouth, the office and church warden of St Martin's Church, Dorking, and Huw Alban Davies.

I am grateful to Nicholas Power for his water colour paintings of knot designs.

Thanks to Marnie Fry for the graphic designs.

I am grateful to Dominic Walters for his photography of Old Place Farm (pp.34, 43, 44, 47 and 59), Horns Lodge (pp.40, 45 and 59) and Troutbeck (front cover and pp.8, 33, 38, 39, 41, 58, 101, 102 and 113).

Photographs were reproduced by kind permission of:

The Sussex Archaeological Society (p.9).
The Collection of Historical Scientific Instruments, Harvard University (p.10).
Dennis Jarvis (p.11).
The Patrick Taylor/RHS Lindley Collections (pp.11, 18, 28, 29 and 37).
The 8th Earl and Countess of Harewood House Trust (p.14).

The Board of Trustees, the Chevening House Estate (pp.16, 19 and 20).
Sudeley Castle and Gardens (p.21).
Lynn Batdorf (pp.67, 76 and 83).
European Boxwood and Topiary Society (pp.120, 130, 132, 133, 135 and 137).
The Sir Harold Hillier Gardens and Arboretum (p.64).
Peter Baistow (pp.20, 100 and 107).
helenfickling.com (pp.97, 101 and 116).
Mick Hales (p.46).
Marianne Majerus, Helmingham Hall (design Xa Tollemache); (p.22) (design André van Wassenhove; (p.55); Sandhill Farm House (design Rosemary Alexander) (p.54).
Andrew Lawson, courtesy of the Garden Museum (p.22).

INTRODUCTION

History of Box in Gardens

Box has been used by gardeners since the earliest times, probably for at least 6,000 years. Egyptian palaces had pleasure gardens with clipped box plants to mark out elaborate designs. Drawings of these gardens were even placed in the tombs of the privileged dead to remind them of the joys they could anticipate in the afterlife. The Romans also valued box as a structural component of a formal garden in their villas and palaces. Pliny the Younger wrote about his villa at Laurentum, situated on the coast south-west of Rome, describing shaded paths bordered by hedges, ornamental parterres and bushes of box plants trimmed to ornamental shapes in the form of animals. The Romans took their appreciation for box with them as they carried their civilization to the furthest parts of their empire. The excavations at Fishbourne Palace in West Sussex uncovered remnants of box wood near the remains of bedding trenches that bordered a wide path, with straight lines embellished with semi-circular and rectangular recesses. These parterres may well have been cultivated from locally grown plants because *Buxus* is a species native to Britain.

The formal garden of a first-century AD Roman palace has been reconstructed at Fishbourne, West Sussex, where remnants of *Buxus* were found in the elaborate bedding trenches. Box hedging has been planted according to the original plan.

Quite apart from box's attraction to gardeners, the plant itself was held almost in reverence in the past. This was because of a connection to funereal rites inspired by the symbolic character of its leaves, which long withstand decay, and also possibly because box-wood has a particularly dense and heavy texture making it suitable for fashioning into objects for fine engraving, such as intricately carved figures and boxes used to store precious items. Box has been used by craftsmen in a number of specialized areas on account of its fine grain, which makes it useful for precision work. Box is also extremely tenacious due to its high density, which varies from 0.85 to 1.13kg per cubic metre, and this makes it heavy enough to sink in water. Box was particularly appreciated by the makers of musical instruments and woodwinds were often made from boxwood, which was known for its highly refined and smooth sound pattern. It was also used for chin-rests, tailpieces and pegs in violins, and by the makers of scientific instruments for navigational and measuring devices. There are references to boxwood in Homer's *The Iliad*, which mentions its use for the yoke of Priam's horses, and also in the Bible, Book of Isiah, 30.8, where Isiah's message was published on tablets made of boxwood. Excavations at King Midas' Gordian Palace in Turkey have revealed more than thirty pieces of furniture that were composed, in part, from box-wood. More authoritative evidence for the illustrious pedigree of box can hardly exist than these examples from posterity.

The Flourishing of Knot Gardens in Tudor Times

The origin of the modern formal garden was in monasteries and country estates in medieval and earlier times, with square or rectangular beds and herbs or medicinal plants growing in the enclosed space. By Tudor times these geometrical forms had become valued for their ornamental, as well as their functional, properties and they evolved into knot gardens, which were grown to be admired for themselves and often situated close to the house and viewed from an upper storey window. Box itself had become unpopular and gained a poor reputation from books such as Charles Estienne's *Maison Rustique* (1586), translated to English by Richard Surflet (1600). He writes that: '... as for boxe in as much as it is of a naughtie smell, it is to be left of and not dealt withal .... It is not to be planted neere the place where bees are kept, for the flower killeth them soddainly. Some affirme that it corrupteth the aire by the stinking smell that it hath, and for this cause it

A Nocturnal instrument made from boxwood. Nocturnals were invented in the sixteenth century and used by mariners to determine the time to an accuracy of 15min by observing the relative positions of two stars. The fine grain of the wood enabled precise markings to be inscribed.

Terminology

A word about the terminology used in this book. *Buxus* is the Latin name for the plant and was adopted by the taxonomist Linnaeus when he gave a name to the genus. I have used *Buxus* when the context is essentially horticultural, elsewhere the more everyday name box is employed because gardeners generally use the colloquial term. This applies in the anglophone world; in North America the colloquial name is 'boxwood'.

would be as sparingly planted in the garden as possible may be.' Knot gardens in the Tudor period were raised with plants such as germander and a variety of herbs. The designs were derived from ideas that were fashionable in decoration at this time, such as strapwork decorations. An example of strapwork is the 1589 panel on the tomb of Sir Gawen Carew in Exeter Cathedral. It has been suggested that the woodblocks that were used by printers in books of designs for embroidery patterns might also have been used in gardening books as models for knot gardens. In support of this, early versions of knot designs do show single lines, as would be expected of a needlework pattern, not double lines with shading, as would be appropriate for a three-dimensional representation of a knot garden. The Elizabethans also used knots to convey meanings that were at times hidden and intended only to be deciphered by those to whom the message was intended, like the 'conceits' expressed in the poetry of the time. Knots were drawn up in heraldic forms with the intention of drawing attention to the status of the owner of the property. The popularity of knot designs continued and box came back into fashion with the Jacobean era. Garden writers such as Gervase Markham were soon to consider box indispensable and it regained its earlier popularity. The most enduring of all the knot designs of this period is perhaps the True Lovers Knott as depicted in Stephen Blake's *The Compleat Gardener's Practice* (1664).

ABOVE: The cloister garden in the monastery of Mont St Michel, Normandy, France. This garden was reconstructed by Benedictine monks as a place of contemplation. The square of box is surrounded by Damask roses and other herbaceous plants.

The box design at Moseley Old Hall, Staffordshire. The design was copied from a drawing of 1640 by Reverend Walter Stonehouse. The use of contrasting materials with sandy gravel for the walkways and larger white stones filling the circular box shapes animates the view, particularly when seen from the upper windows of the house.

The strapwork decoration of Sir Gawen Carew's tomb in Exeter Cathedral. The motif has a marked similarity to some of the designs in contemporary sixteenth-century books used for planning the layout of knots in gardens.

The True Lovers Knott from Stephen Blake's *The Compleat Gardener's Practice* of 1664. There is something sad about Blake's inscription 'Heere I have made the true Lovers Knott To try it in Mariage was never my Lott', but little is known about the man himself apart from the fact that he was the gardener to William Ouglander, a Member of Parliament, and his book, as well as instructing on the methods for maintaining gardens for medicinal, kitchen and pleasure use, had thirty designs for 'beautifying of the garden'.

The Parterre, an Essential of Formal Garden Design

The other important element of formal garden design is the parterre, a space enclosed by hedging with the area inside covered by grass, planting, gravel or a paving material. Parterres were used with great effect during the Renaissance, with the introduction of classical styles of building from the Greek and Roman period, which were founded on symmetry and the manipulation of space and proportions. It is not surprising that the gardens of the grand palaces that were built in Italy from the fifteenth-century onward, by architects such as Brunelleschi, and subsequently copied elsewhere in Europe, reflected the geometrical features of the buildings that they were created to complement. Box was the perfect medium to translate these concepts into the formal gardens that were laid out in front of the main facade of the grand house, with the approach flanked by symmetrical formations of parterres outlined by neatly clipped box hedges leading to the grand entrance. Sited in symmetrical positions in the parterres were pieces of topiary, usually trimmed box in elaborate shapes, which reflected

the statues carved from stone set into the facade of the grand house, denoting the majesty of its owner. This classical style of gardening made a major impact in England in the late-seventeenth century when William of Orange introduced the formal box garden from Holland, his native country, where it had been popular for some time. He redesigned the privy garden at Hampton Court along classical lines and the style was soon taken up elsewhere in the country.

The Romantic Period

In England at the beginning of the eighteenth century there was a strong movement voiced by the author Alexander Pope and the diarist Joseph Addison, which

The grand parterre in front of the Upper Belvedere Palace, Vienna. Prince Eugene of Savoy commissioned Dominique Girard to plan these formal gardens, which extend on descending ground to the Lower Belvedere Palace.

ridiculed what they saw as the artificial contortions of topiary and classical forms, in favour of a more natural type of gardening. The new style of the landscape park followed the inherent aspects of the land with paths following natural contours, rather than the straight lines of geometric designs. Carefully situated features, such as copses and water courses, were introduced to give structure and interest when viewed from a distance, and the overall design took advantage of natural features beyond the park. For instance, an avenue might be cut through a wood to allow a view of a distant church spire. Landscape gardening reached its apogee with the most successful garden designer of the era, Lancelot 'Capability' Brown. Instead of the statues, topiary and fountains of the formal period, the furnishings of this new style were romantic pieces of architecture, such as grottos, follies and bridges, placed to accentuate the picturesque qualities of the scene. However, at the turn of the eighteenth century, the more intimate style of gardening came back to favour with designers such as Humphry Repton who responded to their clients' desire for a more convivial, immediate setting for their houses, rather than having

rolling parkland up to the front door itself. For this reason, terraces, balustrades and flower gardens, often with box parterres, came back into fashion, together with the ha-ha, a fosse dug at the perimeter of the garden that prevented farm animals and deer from the park from encroaching on the domestic area of the house.

Victorian Times to the Modern Day

During the Victorian era there was an appreciation for detail and exoticism in the more modest gardens seen in village houses. This reflected some of the features seen in the grander establishments that were built at the time and in this way box, in the form of topiary as well as knots and parterres, became an egalitarian feature, with gardeners wanting to introduce a picturesque look to their own garden. In the previous century, the popularity of box was sustained, with the interest renewed by a series of garden historians and authors who reconnected the ever-growing gardening public to the charms of box in its various forms. After the Second World War, as private country houses were

The view from the Terrace at Harewood House, Yorkshire, which was designed by Charles Barry in about 1840. The magnificent formal parterre overlooks a view of the park, plans for which were drawn up by 'Capability' Brown in 1758–81. This is a superb example of these two styles of garden design.

opened to the public, gardeners could see for themselves the spectacular way that box was put to work and were often inspired to take ideas back to their own homes. Another factor that undoubtedly increased the popularity of box in the present era was its greater availability from nurseries that specialized in supplying plants and topiary. This was particularly the case in Holland, which has a long history of nurturing *Buxus* in all forms suitable for horticulture and was an abundant source of mature topiary, as well as younger plants for hedging.

Box in the Contemporary Garden

Although box is primarily associated with formal gardens, it has recently been used with great effect to fulfil a number of design purposes in the contemporary garden. 'Capability' Brown was fond of surveying a landscape and pointing out how he could 'punctuate' it by introducing a feature, such as a copse of trees. Box will do the same in a small scale with a spectacular topiary shape acting as a full stop at the end of a vista, a series of balls as commas along a border or a pair of spirals as exclamation marks to emphasize an entrance. Box is also used for continuity, cohesion and, at times, for contrast. As an evergreen shrub it has a beautifully stable colour that can give contrast to herbaceous planting and it provides continuity to a changing pattern, as well as life to a garden in winter, particularly when decorated with snow. Modern gardens make use of hedges, often of yew, to separate different parts of the garden into rooms where different themes hold sway. In most circumstances box will not have enough time to grow to serve this purpose but it does introduce structure to the modern garden by giving a pathway a margin to make it more striking, by marking out different gardening themes with perimeter hedging and by edging beds. There are many other examples.

Yew and box topiary outlined by snow, which gives the garden welcome interest in the winter.

Free-Flowing *Buxus*

So far, all mentions of box in gardens have related to its use as topiary or as a very deliberate ornamental, structural feature. However, box also has a role in its own natural form, without any clipping, training or shaping – the actor without any costume or make-up. The genus *Buxaceae* is enormously varied with regard to the colour, shape and size of the leaves, as well as the habit of the plant, which varies from tall and upright to low and spreading. It is not surprising that the species and cultivars of *Buxus* are widely used by gardeners to fill a number of functions, which take advantage of its many attractive forms. A solitary box can be an admired specimen and a group of box plants can strengthen an area of the garden. A box bush can be substantial enough to make a boundary or to introduce variety to a shrubbery; it can also bring contrast by introducing a lighter or darker colour, depending on the need. *Buxus* is a slow-growing genus but, with a mind to posterity, the foresighted gardener does well to plant and nurture a suitable plant that will one day be admired as a tree.

Why *Buxus* is Such a Useful Plant

Buxus has botanical features that make it ideal for a number of roles in both formal and modern gardens, and in many ways there is no substitute. It is resilient and resistant to dry weather conditions. Its slow growth and small, dense foliage make it particularly suited for clipping into topiary and hedging shapes, and this needs to be done only once a year. Faster growing plants do not hold their shape and have to be trimmed frequently during the season. Box can be made into an endless number of forms because it will shoot from the most radical pruning. It can be trained and, after a year or two, it will take up the new shape, making it very suitable for making into a complex topiary figure. Their extreme longevity allows box gardens to endure for centuries. The garden at Levens Hall in Cumbria was laid down between 1689 and 1712 by the French gardener Guillaume de Beaumont, in line with contemporary taste, influenced by William of Orange's appreciation of topiary, so prevalent in his native country, Holland. The magnificent variety of shapes at

The light-coloured, gnarled branches of an aged box tree at Chevening House, Kent.

Levens Hall, some quite outlandish and bizarre, has survived almost completely intact from the 1690s to the present day as a form of horticultural time capsule. Devoted attention by a series of owners, as well as the enduring qualities of *Buxus* itself, were necessary for the preservation of the garden but box, even when completely neglected, can survive by reverting to its native form, which is a dense, slow-growing tree. Such specimens, when rediscovered by a later generation of gardeners, can be enjoyed in that form or converted by imaginative clipping into a massive undulating landscape. Although in many ways the most long-lasting of plants, since the mid-1990s *Buxus* has proved itself to be vulnerable to diseases, which have been introduced to Western Europe. These diseases, primarily box blight *Calonectria henricotiae/C. pseudonaviculata* and the box tree moth, *Cydalima perspectalis*, can be devastating to *Buxus* at all stages of growth. There is no doubt that these diseases make the management of box more difficult and the gardener has to be alert to the problems that can affect the box garden and take prompt steps to counteract them. The husbandry of box in what often seems to be a hostile environment is an issue that is important to any gardener who has the plant or is thinking about planting it, and it is one that is dealt with in this book.

The Approach of This Book

The approach of this book is essentially practical. The gardener who wants to use box as a major feature, in the form of a knot or a parterre, and has not embarked on an ambitious project of this type before, will find information about the techniques and materials that are required, as well as the care necessary for their new project to prosper. It is also written for the gardener who wants no formal features in the garden and would like to use box in one of the many other ways for which it is so well suited. It is hoped that this book will take the gardener who is new to box to the stage where they are quite confident with handling all aspects of its horticulture, from taking cuttings to training, clipping and nurturing. At the same time, the experienced gardener who may not have come across all aspects of using box will hopefully find something in this book that is of value to them, whether in the way that box can be used to bring out character in areas of a garden that might otherwise be lacking, or in other ways that box can complement a design. I have tried to condense many years of experience of looking after box into straightforward advice about how to keep plants in good condition, how to accurately diagnose incipient problems and how to restore plants to health when affected by infestation, disease, poor nutrition or other circumstances. Box diseases have become more important in recent years and I have brought together the best contemporary advice about how to avoid and control these problems in a holistic way. Responsible use of pathogen controls is essential, but natural husbandry, combined with careful observation and patience, is a vitally important but often neglected part of the armamentarium.

Box has an enduring value for gardeners. With an allowance for the cycles of fashion, it has given pleasure for almost as long as gardens have been planned and cultivated by gardeners. Gardens with box are invariably full of character and atmosphere and they have a sense of calmness and tranquillity. Box plays its part by giving the garden stability throughout the year, with the flow of a repeating horizontal shape drawing the eye and linking the garden to the surrounding landscape. When the winter garden is dormant, the clean, evergreen lines of box stand proud and bring permanence, while the clipped shapes become a sturdy platform for a covering of frost or snow, giving the garden a magical atmosphere. By June, those same shapes blend with the exuberance of summer and play a different role, combining with other elements in the garden to produce a balanced and complementary whole.

CHAPTER 1

USING BOX IN FORMAL GARDEN DESIGN

The Principles of Introducing Formal Structure

Formal planting, when done successfully, will make balance and structure an important element in the overall design and bring the house and the garden into harmony. The house and its views will determine how to coordinate the building with the garden and how to set the atmosphere of the garden. It is also important that the formal area should be designed in such a way that there are links to the surrounding terrain and, where relevant, to the land beyond.

If the house is surrounded by a sufficiently large area of garden, it is necessary, first of all, to plan how to design the main paths and vistas. The direction of these axes will be influenced by the compatibility of the house with the garden, but it is important to bear in mind how the garden is to be used and where to site any areas that are required for sitting and entertaining, as well as a lawn. The connections between these nodes and the natural vistas will largely determine how to plan the area for formal planting and it is also helpful to look out from the house to find the perspectives that connect it with the garden. Once the structure has been defined, areas of different sorts can be designed with parterres or knots, perhaps with the addition of features such as a sundial, an urn or topiary as the

The magnificent parterre at Chevening House, Kent was originally laid out in around 1820 by the 4th Earl Stanhope. It was re-planted to the designs of Elizabeth Banks in the 1970s. The box-edged beds are filled by a paisley pattern of bedding plants and coloured herbs.

focus for a smaller formal area. In addition, simple lines of formality, like box edging or topiary box balls, can lead away from the house into other parts of the garden that are hidden from sight, where new domains open up and catch the viewer's eye with a delightful element of surprise. Here would be a place to pause

Detail of the parterre at Chevening House showing lavender and cotton lavender (*Santolina chamaecyparissus*) planted in between box scrolls.

and contemplate, and could be an ideal position to lay out a small knot, particularly if your garden has a change in level and there is a possibility of taking advantage of the view from above.

Knot Gardens

Planning a Knot Garden

Drawings of the ornamental knot gardens of the six-teenth and seventeenth centuries show that the patterns were based on a square, and during the Tudor period, when they enjoyed great popularity, they were planted with herbs such as germander, hyssop and winter savoury. The designs of knots were derived from the decorative arts where patterns would be found in embroidery work, carpets, stonework and elaborate ceiling plaster mouldings. Box was out of fashion during the Tudor period but soon regained the popularity it had enjoyed during earlier times and has been chosen for knot gardens ever since then because there is no other hedging plant that can be kept to a low level and clipped with such precision. Box is

A circular box garden with an urn as a centrepiece, which links with the parterre beyond. The formality is softened by the early summer flowering of roses.

renowned for its strong structure and will hold its shape after it is clipped. This is seen all the year round but particularly in winter when a heavy snowfall will lie on the hedge or topiary and its strength will give a solid platform without collapsing. Throughout the year, the colour will remain consistently dark green, apart from the lighter green of early spring growth. Longevity is a key factor when choosing box, as it will give many years of pleasure after the careful and time-consuming process of laying out a knot garden.

When deciding on what area of ground to position a knot, it is useful to remember that, although box can thrive in most conditions, it is best to plant a knot garden in an area with an open aspect that has sun and dappled shade. A simple knot will require very little annual maintenance and only needs a programme of ground maintenance, including mulching, when appropriate and a single clip during the summer. There are no rules about the measurements of a knot garden, although the usual size is approximately 3–4m² (32–43ft²). Every case is individual and the designer has to consider what is correct for the chosen place in the garden. A knot happily stands alone and is enjoyed for the complexity and symmetry of its lines, although standard roses or topiary can be used to add variation and height. A small knot garden is intricate and the woven shape may not allow for interior planting. Not only would planting confuse the pattern but it would also crowd the box and

possibly cause damage to it. For this reason, pea shingle or sand is usually laid as a background to the pattern. If the desire is to have a small design that incorporates perennials and bulbs, then choose a more open design with fewer interlinking hedges and more space for planting, but still with a symmetry of design. Most gardeners find that clipping and maintaining a knot is an enjoyable and therapeutic job, as the 'over and under' lines of the various coloured box are trimmed and the cross-over points kept flowing.

Buxus sempervirens 'Suffruticosa' was often recommended as the cultivar to choose for knot gardens; however, it is slow-growing and the plant's habit is compact and dense, which makes it more vulnerable to disease – particularly box blight. Also, individual 'Suffruticosa' plants, with their rounded habit, will take longer to join together as a mature hedge. For these reasons, a better choice for knot gardens is common box, *B. sempervirens*, with the coloured cultivars *B. sempervirens* 'Elegantissima' and *B. sempervirens* 'Latifolia Maculata' used to provide contrast in the design, if required.

Creating a Knot Garden

There is every reason why a gardener should choose a knot design that dates from the time when a great deal of creative thought went into their composition. It is

The beautiful knot design at Sudeley Castle in the Cotswold Hills, Gloucestershire. The design is based on a pattern of a dress worn by Queen Elizabeth I in a portrait, *The Allegory of the Tudor Succession*, which hangs in the castle.

A knot design at Helmingham Hall, Suffolk. The interlinking design is loose enough to allow sufficient space for spring planting.

certainly true that the works of Elizabethan and Jacobean designers are no less successful when re-created today. Examples of knots laid to these designs can be visited in gardens open to the public, and a knowledge of their provenance can add to the enjoyment of reproducing one in your own garden.

The gardener may also be inspired to create a design of their own by drawing geometric shapes on a piece of graph paper before laying them out on the ground to a suitable scale. Alternatively, the design might be free-form; for instance, a unique shape made up from the initials of the couple who own the garden. Books of calligraphy containing elaborate lettering make the design more interesting, particularly if they are intertwined in a

suitable way. There is an endless number of possibilities, but any arrangement that can be drawn to scale and transposed to your site is suitable for a knot. A particular delight of the knot garden is that its creator starts with a design on paper, plans the steps necessary to realize it on the ground and, finally, when the terrain is measured, the ground prepared and planting done, stands back and watches as the original concept matures into a reality. This is a great pleasure and not diminished because the rewards are some time in their realization.

Laying out a knot garden can be a challenging, although an invariably rewarding, undertaking. In this section, the designs for two knots are given. They can both be planted without the need for laying out elaborate

An example of *The True Lovers Knott*, a design based on Stephen Blake's *The Compleat Gardener's Practice* of 1664 (knot to the left of picture). The other knot is based on a design in *La Maison Rustique* (1583) by Charles Estienne. This knot garden was planted at Barnsley House in Gloucestershire. Barnsley House was the home of Rosemary Verey, the internationally renowned garden designer and writer.

Monograms made from the initials of the owners of a house have been a feature of garden design since Tudor times. Here they make a striking approach to the front door.

Techniques for Transposing Designs to the Ground

3, 4, 5 Technique for Drawing Right Angles

Most knot designs require a rectilinear shape. It is essential that the right angles are drawn true or errors will accumulate and the figure will be lop-sided.

1. Mark a line 4 units long (a unit is any convenient length).
2. Using a tape-measure, measure out 3 units at an approximate perpendicular from the end of the line and leave the tape-measure in place.
3. With another tape-measure, measure 5 units from the other end of the line and adjust the two tape-measures until they meet. The perpendicular line is now an exact rectangle (90 degrees).

The 3, 4, 5 technique for drawing right angles.

continued overleaf

Techniques for Transposing Designs to the Ground *continued*

Drawing Planting Lines in the Soil with a Sand Compass

Drawing lines for planting is made easier with a trace of sand on the ground.

1. Drill a hole in the cap of a used liquid bottle, so that sand flows through at a rate suitable for leaving a trace on prepared soil; a 6mm (¼in) hole is generally satisfactory. Make sure that the sand is dry.
2. To draw a circle or an arc, tie string around the neck of the bottle and attach to a stick at the centre of the radius.
3. Hold the bottle at an angle to deliver a good flow of sand with the string taught.

Drawing planting lines in the soil with a sand compass.

grids and framework. To be accurate and symmetrical it is necessary to draw some geometrical shapes on the ground and the simple plans for these are shown, together with the watercolour drawings of the finished knot designs, so that the planting schemes are made clear. First of all, the basic techniques for laying out knot designs on the ground are described.

More Complicated Knot Designs

If a more elaborate design of knot is required, it is suggested that you consult a book with specimen knot gardens, or drawings of knots, and pick one that suits your taste. Books from garden designers of the classical period in the seventeenth century have been re-printed, such as William Lawson's *The Countrie Housewifes Garden*, 1617 (published by Breslich & Foss, 1983 from Lawson's 3rd edition). Contemporary books that may also provide suitable designs include

Knot Gardens and Parterres by Robin Whalley and Anne Jennings (1998) and *Classic Garden Design* by Rosemary Verey (1984). The basic techniques for creating more complicated knot gardens follows:

1. Measure out your land and make a drawing on graph paper to a suitable scale.
2. Mark out the site by setting up a square outline with pegs. In most cases, the pegs should be at intervals of a half metre (1½ft), and string is then stretched between the pegs to make a grid of squares that corresponds with your scale drawing, enabling you to transpose the shapes from your scale model to the ground.
3. Next, put in pegs to mark out centres of the design and important intersections.
4. Lines for planting are marked with a sand bottle and the arcs of circles and semi-circles can be drawn using a sand-bottle compass.

A Design Based on a Knot in *La Maison Rustique* (1583) by Charles Estienne

This design was popularized by Gervase Markham in his book *The Countrie Farm*.

1. Having chosen your position on the ground, draw a square of the required size. The dimensions of the plan are 3 × 3 units but this can be modified to anything you require by working out the ratio between the given and the required values.
2. Next, tap in pegs and connect with string, as shown by black lines in the layout diagram.
3. Using the sand bottle, mark out the planting lines, as shown by the lines in the coloured planting plan. Draw semi-circles at A with a radius 50cm (20in); circles at B with radius 27cm (10½in) and a circle at C with radius 46cm (18in). Rub out the traces of sand at the intersections where one type of *Buxus* gives way to another.
4. Plants should be spaced at 25cm (10in) distance. For instructions about preparation of the soil, *see* Chapter 5. When the hedges have grown they should be clipped to a width of 25cm (10in).

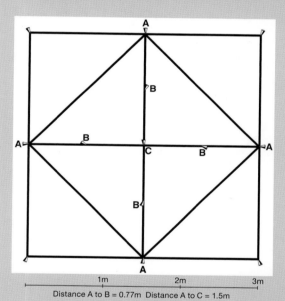

1m   2m   3m

Distance A to B = 0.77m Distance A to C = 1.5m

ABOVE: Plan for drawing sand lines for planting three colours of box.

ABOVE LEFT: Diagram for laying out string lines on ground for *La Maison Rustique* knot.

LEFT: Water-colour painting for *La Maison Rustique* knot to show the planting pattern of *Buxus sempervirens* (mid-green), *B. sempervirens* 'Elegantissima' (dark green) and 'Latifolia Maculata' (gold).

A Knot Design Based on a Drawing from the *Countrie Housewifes Garden* (1617) by William Lawson

The dimensions of the plan are 3 × 3m (10 × 10ft), but these can be adapted by adjusting the ratios of the scale.

1. Tap in pegs and stretch lines between them as in the layout diagram.
2. Use the sand bottle to mark out the planting lines. Use a sand compass to draw semi-circles of radius 75cm (29½in) at points A. Rub out the traces of sand at the intersections where one type of *Buxus* gives way to another. *See* the coloured planting plan.
3. Plants should be spaced at 25cm (10in) distance. For instructions about preparation of the soil, *see* Chapter 5. When the hedges have grown, they should be clipped to a width of 25cm (10in). This design could be combined with internal planting.

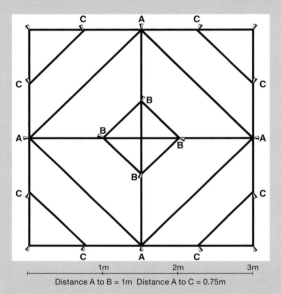

Distance A to B = 1m Distance A to C = 0.75m

ABOVE: Plan for drawing sand lines for planting three colours of box.

ABOVE LEFT: Diagram for laying out string lines on ground for *Countrie Housewifes Garden* knot.

LEFT: Water-colour painting for *The Countrie Housewifes Garden* knot to show the pattern of planting pattern of *Buxus sempervirens* (mid-green), *B. sempervirens* 'Elegantissima' (dark green) and 'Latifolia Maculata' (gold).

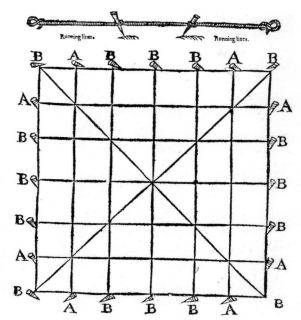

Woodcut from Charles Estienne's seventeenth-century *Maison Rustique* showing a grid for laying out a knot using pegs and string. In Estienne's words: 'You shall have in your hand many measures of small cord re-reeles and dibbles … and stretch your line to draw and cast the shape of it … to dispose them such as may delight the eie …'. For this technique, nothing has changed since Estienne's day.

Before drawing the shape of the knot on the ground, the soil needs to be prepared for planting, this is discussed in Chapter 5. If the knot design is planted in either grass or gravel, a simple brick or stone surround is an elegant and useful way of ensuring that grass or gravel does not encroach on the design.

Parterres

A parterre is an outlined shape or a design made up from a number of shapes on level ground. It is generally arranged in a symmetrical pattern and may have intersecting paths that connect with the garden. The format of parterres is larger than that of knot gardens and they are laid out in any form to suit the design, and are edged by box with the internal space filled in various ways to complement the particular style. According to the classification used by garden designers in the classical age of formal gardens in the eighteenth century, parterres were made in different styles.

Types of Parterres

Cutwork and Embroidery Parterres
These are symmetrical designs of beds edged by box and separated by paths of aggregate material. They are often filled with flowers and the planting scheme can be changed with the seasons if annual planting is used. In the more elaborate examples, the predominant shapes were free-flowing forms of a lace-like pattern, referred to as parterres of embroidery. The word 'cutwork' is, in fact, from a needlework technique in which a portion of a textile is cut away and the space filled with embroidery or needle lace.

Parterre à l'Anglaise
Parterres à l'anglaise feature mown grass with box hedge borders. These shapes were also laid simply as lawns, without the hedge border, because of the difficulty of mowing the grass close to hedging.

Scrollwork and Knot Parterres
In scrollwork parterres, the complexity of the design is as intricate as in formal knot gardens, with interlocking whirls of clipped box weaving a complicated pattern. Allied to the scrollwork parterre is the knot parterre in which the compact knot format is elongated from a square into a larger rectangular shape, so that colourful annual planting can be laid out in the spaces.

Other Design Features Used in Parterres
Unlike knots, which are laid out in a symmetrical, geometric pattern with intersecting lines intertwined and overlapped, most types of parterre have a freer shape and, although symmetry was also an essential feature, there were many other devices in the hands of the designer to decorate the inside of these parterres. They included curlicues, leaf-like scrolling known as branch-work and swirling shapes derived from embroidery designs. Unlike knots there are no set-piece designs copied and used by generations of gardeners; parterres are more individual. A large parterre that is intricately constructed will only be a success if the site chosen is in harmony with its surrounds, as the detail of the design can overpower a smaller garden. The empty space around the parterre

The embroidery parterre at Oxburgh Hall, Norfolk. It dates from the Victorian era and was planted in 1845 from a design for *Parterres de Broderie* from John James' *Theory and Practice of Gardening*, 1712. The compartments are filled with permanent planting and summer bedding.

The North-East Parterre at Pitmedden, Aberdeenshire, was based on a seventeenth-century design from Holyrood House. The original house was destroyed by fire in the early-nineteenth century, but the four elaborate parterres are maintained to a meticulous standard and 60,000 annual bedding plants are used in the parterres and planted between the elaborate scrollwork.

becomes an important part of the whole design, as it is essential to have that balance and to be able to stand back and enjoy the view of the parterre. In a smaller area, the success of the parterre will depend on how it is incorporated into the flow of the garden. With some small patterns, box ball standards on a single stem or sculptural box topiary planted at intervals will give the necessary punctuation to make a quiet design into something more elegant. If the intention is to plant the compartments of the parterre, then choose a planting plan that will not overwhelm the distinct lines of the box hedging. When space is limited, the choice should be a compact flowering plant. However, flowing perennials can be successful as long as the design of the parterre allows enough planting space in between the hedging. What must be avoided is for any lush summer growth to lie on the box as this is unsightly and may possibly damage the box.

The elaborate embroidery parterres laid out in the gardens of historic houses are inspiring but would not transfer to many gardens today. However, it may be possible to reproduce a detail of the pattern and fit it, in the correct scale, to a larger town or country garden. The patterns of the embroidery style are elaborate and by filling with flowers between the lines of box, the design becomes delightful and extremely decorative, particularly a scrollwork or cutwork parterre sited close to the house and planted with appropriate annuals where it can be enjoyed from a terrace or an upper room. It was during the Victorian period that plant breeders hybridized annuals to give more colour, uniform height and a longer flowering season, and this was suitable for carpet bedding in the parterres that became fashionable at that time. Today, there is a spectacular colour range of annuals to choose from and a seasonal planting programme could use autumn, spring and summer bedding, possibly underplanted by bulbs to give additional autumn and spring interest. However, even a small design of this sort would require large numbers of small plants and a good deal of labour to manage successfully and it would be more costly to maintain than other parterres that have a permanent planting of perennials. The reward would be a romantic pattern with a chance to introduce an intense and strong colour scheme to the garden, which varied with the seasons. This form of gardening is versatile and would give an opportunity to plant a special display with a lavish palette of bedding plants for an event such as a wedding or an anniversary

Choosing a Design for a Parterre

The designs for parterres are much more individual than are those for knots and if the ambition is to create this form, look for inspiration in books of classical parterres and for photographs of current examples. Once a design has been found, make a scale drawing on graph paper and carefully measure out the land,

The small parterre at Mottisfont Abbey, Hampshire, was designed by the socialite garden designer Norah Lindsay in 1938, using the fanlight of the door of the house as a model. The paths are lined with dwarf lavender and varied seasonal planting. Here, dark-red antirrhinums are planted together with *Heliotropium × hybridum* 'Cherry Pie' and *Verbena × hybrida*.

making sure not only that it fits, but that there is a suitable margin around it to site it comfortably without crowding. The basic technique is similar to that for laying out knots, although more complex because of the often elaborate shapes and the larger scale of the undertaking.

The Parterre at Restoration House

The re-creation of the parterre at Restoration House in Rochester, Kent, is an example of how the concept for a box design can be inspired by the history of its particular setting – ideas from the past brought imaginatively to life through the medium of box. Restoration House takes its name from King Charles II's sojourn in Rochester on his way from Dover to London in 1660, where he was to be restored to the throne as the successor to his beheaded father. The garden's history is older and excavation by the present owners, Jonathan Wilmot and Robert Tucker, uncovered remains of Tudor walls that enclose a rectangular area with an overlooking mount. Enormous efforts were taken to restore the garden from a state of ruin, and research by the garden historian, Elizabeth Hall, suggested that the mount was a viewing point for the area beneath, which is likely to have contained a parterre, in line with the ideas of garden designers of the time. There is no historical source for the design of the parterre but inspiration for the owners was close at hand in a type of pattern that we know was an influence to the creators of parterres of the time. The strapwork style of decoration that was used in parterres was also used in mouldings for ceilings, in embroidery designs, as well as in woodwork. It happens that the fine wooden door to the rear of the house, which faces the garden, was constructed with intricate strapwork panelling that had been in place since the seventeenth century, making it a contemporary of the original garden. The design of this door was copied and used as a model for the twentieth-century parterre, laid down in the 1990s. The parterre is maintained with great care and clipped annually by hand.

The parterre at Restoration House, Rochester, Kent. The gardens have been painstakingly restored to as near their original state as careful historical research allows. Enormous obstacles, including unauthorized modern housing developments, had to be removed to restore the tranquillity of this delightful place, which is situated in the middle of a bustling city.

The seventeenth-century panelled wooden door at the rear of the house. The design was taken as the model for the contemporary parterre.

Topiary in Formal Garden Design

Topiary is the art of clipping plants, shrubs and trees into ornamental shapes to give the appearance of living sculpture. Box, particularly *Buxus sempervirens*, is an outstanding evergreen plant with an ideal structure for making into topiary because of its great ability to rejuvenate after extensive pruning and there is no other small evergreen plant that can be clipped to such a fine finish. There are other species and cultivars of *Buxus* that have faster growth, but because of their larger and coarser leaves and less dense structure, they will not clip as finely as *B. sempervirens*.

In a formal garden, topiary has several roles that it can perform to set the stage and create the required atmosphere. An example of this is the way that topiary can reinforce an entrance when planted on either side of the opening to herald the way into another area of the garden. This has been done at Sissinghurst Castle where box spheres play an architectural role on either side of a walled entrance leading into the rose garden. A simple dome or pyramid, when repeated in different parts of the garden, will draw your eye and pull the whole design together. The effect of repeated planting of topiary shapes is both structural and ornamental, and a formal line of identical topiary, clipped to a geometric shape, performs the same purpose as a hedge,

The parterre at Restoration House, which was planted in 1994 on the reclaimed site of what was thought to be a Tudor parterre.

A watchful bird holds its own against strong shapes of yew.

without the hardness of line. The strength of box topiary is that the recurrent shapes give clarity to the way the garden holds together and they bring elegance to the design. The art of gardening with topiary is to incorporate the various domains that are present, each with its own style, and to link them by means of repetitive shapes and a uniform colour. Different parts of a garden need connecting in some order and this is where subtle formality with topiary and hedging can smooth the transition from one area to another. At the early stages of designing a garden that is to include topiary, it is helpful to position a stake in all the places where individual pieces might play a pivotal role. In this way, the potential positions for topiary can be viewed from many angles and by using this simple method you can become confident with your placement.

Topiary shapes have the presence to act on their own when a strong focal point is required. They are used with advantage in knot and parterre gardens when elegant shapes, such as multiple tiers or standards, act as the centrepiece or mark out key points in the design. A vertical piece of solitary topiary set into the centre of a bed will give a strong sense of formality and would rival an urn in a similar setting. The clipped shape will catch the early morning light and the soft evening shadows later in the day. The topiary can take any form that is in tune with the overall design and this could be a complex tier or a geometric shape, such as an obelisk. The repetition of an eye-catching upright form can be used in a small, formal setting or deployed in a substantial knot such as that at Moseley Old Hall (pictured in the Introduction) where eight standard box with spherical crowns give a magnificent perpendicular dimension to the design.

CHAPTER 2

BOX IN CONTEMPORARY GARDEN DESIGN

The Less Traditional Approach

In formal gardens, the role of box is predominant and will heavily influence how the other parts contribute to the overall design. In a contemporary garden, such a powerful use of formal planting is not usually desired, although smaller formal areas can be incorporated without dominating. Nevertheless, box is an invaluable tool for the imaginative designer looking for a less traditional approach, because it can be used to achieve important effects in a number of ways. One of the strengths of box is that it can be sculpted and moulded into different shapes, giving the designer the option to contrast, support and emphasize other elements. In the past, box was associated with the construction of parterres and knots, and it was also used in walled vegetable gardens where enclosures of hedging marked out the beds. In contemporary design, box has been put to use in a great many more ways.

Box is used by the modern designer to link one part of the garden with another and to provide continuity between different areas. Box hedging is also able to define and separate areas of the garden that are set aside for different purposes. Box is particularly useful when there is no need to shut off the space that has been created from the rest of the garden because it is clipped to a low level. Box topiary can serve as a punctuation mark, indicating the change from one style to the next, or as the termination of a theme in the design. The right pieces of box topiary can give an entrance or a walkway a special significance and help to create an atmosphere when proceeding through the gate or along the path. When planted in a massive form, box performs a bold, sculptural role and this can be used either in a naturalistic fashion in the heart of the garden, or when placed alongside a building it can be used to balance an architectural feature. Used in this fashion, box can give strength and solidity in a way that is soft enough to avoid the suggestion of formality.

Level Change

Changes in level of the ground are an asset to the designer because they can be highlighted to become an important feature of the garden and used as a key feature in the composition. A series of steps will catch the eye and can be made more notable by highlighting with box planting to give a clear indication of the rise and fall of the ground. This could be done with items of simple topiary, such as pairs of cones, pyramids or dome shapes at the top and bottom. Alternatively, by using a mass planting of box on either side of the steps

The shape of the two steps is mirrored by the curve of the clipped box, which frames the entrance to the nut walk and reflects the informality of this area of the garden.

it is possible to give the visual impression of a solid bannister that supports the steps and strengthens the impact of what might be a small change of level. Another way that hedging can be used to emphasize a change of level is by planting a box hedge at the side of the slope running up in a curve. Grown to the height of the slope at the bottom, with the height gradually diminishing as it approaches the top, it has the effect of making the slope into a feature in its own right.

Informal Continuity

Two areas of the garden can be connected in an informal way by using box planting to lead between them with a series of simple topiary shapes, such as spheres or cubes. This could be along a defined path but it is also effective when marking the way along an open area. This latter approach is attractive if it takes a curved route, following the contour of the ground, or when it skirts around another garden feature in a meandering direction, avoiding the direct approach of a more formal design that employs linear trimmed hedging. The eye looks for order, and repeated geometrical shapes provide it with visual cues that are picked up unconsciously and lead on to what follows. An example of this is a succession of box spheres along a path through an informal area that connects two more formal parts of the garden. Even when a straight direction cannot be avoided, it is possible to mitigate the orthodoxy of a conventional hedge by using a more complicated geometric form. A good example of box used in this way is shown at Erddig Hall, Wrexham, where a Grecian key motif brings a sense of wit and subtle formality into this delightful avenue.

Mass Effect

Mass planting is a type of land sculpture and this method of using box can be employed in a number of ways in the garden. *Buxus sempervirens* has a natural tendency to form rounded shapes and this can be exploited to make flowing, naturalistic figures. Box can also be cut to precise, geometric precision and when grown in a mass this has an architectural character that a designer can use to mimic hard landscaping in the garden; it is also often used in urban designs.

A striking and very popular use of the mass planting of box in the naturalistic style is the laying down of an undulating shape fashioned in the form of billows of clouds or primeval tumuli. Sometimes these constructions feature half-formed primitive beasts, which generate a feeling of undefined mystery. These

Box balls alternate with clipped lavender to line the curve of the lawn and edge the stone pathway under the rose-clad wooden pergola. The repetitive shapes of the topiary produce a visual effect of continuity and reinforce this strong feature of the garden.

shapes make areas of interest, particularly with the play of shadows as the evening light falls on the irregular forms.

There are many examples of the landscaping function of mass-planted box. A ramp of box can be used to emphasize a subtle change of level in the contour of the ground or to introduce a new area of the garden by leading around from one area to another. There are places in a garden where box can be planted *en masse* to provide informal structure in support of some other feature. In this way it can be used as a background, providing contrast for a planting scheme or a floral border. The evergreen colour of box is a welcome foil to otherwise busy planting.

The qualities of straight-cut box are particularly suited to modern building in an urban environment when a simple geometric block of box is often used as a piece of natural architecture. Green is a colour that is well known to have a restful effect and a block of mass-planted box is refreshing. This is easily achieved with small plants in a grid form and then clipped to shape. A particular example of mass effect is when box is planted in a rectangle and trimmed in a series of steps to form a ziggurat. This shape, with its matt green, fine-textured horizontal and vertical planes makes a green sculpture that will look good when positioned to complement an architectural feature of the house or a garden building. Box planting can also

The straight line of the Irish yew and the corresponding trained fruit trees have an interesting border of box planted in a key motif at Erddig Hall.

A line of box balls, clipped with hand shears, in front of a brick and flint wall with wisteria.

play a role in integrating the garden with the house in a more flowing shape. When a garden area is planted close to the building, the curves of a large box shape can be used to harmonize the two: the solid but asymmetrical form of the box softening the uprights of the house.

Framing

Entrances are enormously important as they create an air of expectation and the style of the planting design on either side of the opening will inevitably anticipate what lies ahead. The approach that is most often taken is to plant a pair of sentinel topiary pieces on either

A mass of trimmed and moulded box cut in unformed shapes, which suggest some indistinct primeval forms. The effect is particularly striking in the evening when shadows fall across the contours.

A solid bank of box is planted as a transition between a formal area with a box parterre and a mound with a grove containing a small statue. The mass planting reflects the shape of the slope and it leads on to the next area of the garden.

A clipped wedge-shape of *Buxus sempervirens* 'Latifolia Maculata' supports the approach to a bridge in an informal part of the garden.

side, choosing the topiary carefully in the light of the impression that it is desired to create. Framing in this way gives the feeling of order and calm formality and also creates a sense of drama for what is on the other side of the opening. This will work well, but an equally imaginative and powerful use of box for framing is shown at the entrance of a house near Penshurst in Kent where a number of different box topiary shapes are planted on either side of the front door. The curves of the different forms complement each other and no

A mass of clipped box forms one side of an enclosed area of garden alongside the house.

A view across the cobbled yard to an opening framed by two box squares with domes, leading to the garden. The symmetry of the clipped shapes composes the entrance to the garden at Comberton near Cambridge.

dissonance is present to disrupt the harmony. The effect is to frame the stone entrance and, together with the two myrtle trees set back on either side, they have a pastoral effect that brings the garden right up to the house.

Framing with a pair of topiary shapes can be a useful way to create a special feature in the garden. An ornamental seat, a piece of sculpture or an ornament, when flanked in this way will become a focus of interest that can be one of the hubs of the overall design. The idea of framing also applies to single objects such as statues or trees, particularly when it is intended that they should be a focal point in the garden. An attractive way to do this is to give the object a circular surround with two colours of box, in a suitable design.

Structure in the Garden

One of the keynotes in the planning of gardens is the construction of rooms for separate areas where different themes prevail. The themes may be distinct types of planting, a particular design, such as a water feature, or a separate function, such as an area for sitting and eating. To separate one room from another requires a barrier and this can be achieved in a number of ways, including hard landscaping with brick walls or a softer option, such as a wooden trellis. If a hedge is considered, then a high hedge of clipped yew gives complete seclusion, but this is not always desired, and low box hedging can be used to demarcate between the garden rooms without interrupting the panorama. With box, the entrances to the rooms can be framed

The stone entrance to this house near Penshurst, Kent, is framed by box topiary shapes of many different shapes and sizes with myrtle trees on either side, which all harmonize with an underlying theme.

Buxus sempervirens and *B. sempervirens* 'Latifolia Maculata' are clipped into alternating segments around the base of the hawthorn tree. This gives an interesting textural quality with the play of light and shade on the softly undulating surface. In spring, the new growth of 'Latifolia Maculata' is a striking mottled-yellow.

with topiary shapes that are grown out of the hedge into cones, spirals or balls that give a vertical dimension to the design and add considerably to the interest.

The kitchen garden has been an integral part of the country house in the British Isles over many centuries. These productive areas require the protection of walls against difficult weather conditions and harsh winds, and create a microclimate that permits plants to be grown that would otherwise not have survived. When the kitchen garden was run efficiently by a team of gardeners it worked well but, sadly, this belongs to another era, except in a few houses that are able to support the necessary staff, although the collective memory lives on through histories such as the Lost Gardens of Heligan. However, the contemporary gardener can replicate some of the positive features of

these gardens on a small scale to produce vegetables and flowers for the house and modern methods can make it entirely manageable. The idea of an enclosure for growing vegetables and plants is an enduring one and, although box hedging will do little as a wind break, it can reproduce the idea of a reserved space for a special purpose

Vistas

Having a vista in a garden adds a sense of drama and exaggerates the dimension of an otherwise unexploited outlook. It will give the garden an axis that will necessarily determine how other design features fit in, so the vista has to be put in at an early stage of planning. The most obvious way to introduce a vista is by employing the technique of 'borrowed' landscape.

The old mansion at Falconhurst has an unusual planting of garden rooms – in this case a quite literal one. The box hedges have been laid down to show how the rooms were arranged in the house before it was destroyed by fire and taken down in the 1960s. Represented are a panelled drawing-room, a south-facing library and a gun room on the north side.

A beautiful and productive contemporary kitchen garden bounded by a brick barn and two sunken greenhouses. There is a strong symmetry of the garden buildings and the house beyond. The box compartments are planted with vegetables and flowers and the octagonal pool is framed by box with integrated balls that strengthen the effect of the design.

The pleached hedge and line of box balls point to the landscape beyond and with the elegant bench they emphasize the force of the vista made from these elements. The power of this device is that the rural hillside becomes part of the garden.

To do this you need to have a suitable prospect visible from the garden. A landmark, such as a church spire or a statuesque tree, might serve as the focal point. A series of simple box shapes, such as balls or cubes, planted as pairs making an avenue that points toward the feature, will create the necessary dramatic effect. A single piece of topiary, or perhaps a seat placed at the end of the avenue, will complement this so long as it does not distract from the distant site. If you lack the outside feature, an alternative is to provide your

A vista to a sundial composed of a box parterre with a central pyramid and an avenue of trees, enclosed by a *Leylandii* hedge.

A box onion in the middle of a planting scheme. The regular shapes of the onion in the herbaceous border provide a contrast with the exuberant display.

own focus in the form of a statue, a sundial or perhaps an elegant bench, and create a perspective by means of a series of visual cues leading up to the focal point.

Contrasts

Having a contrast between one element and another in garden design helps to separate the two and, if chosen wisely, it will bring out the distinct character of both of them. Box is very useful in this regard and it can provide contrast in a number of ways. For instance, an informally planted herbaceous area can look too loose and there is at times a danger of it appearing rather chaotic without some structure to support it. If a number of box shapes are added in a deliberate but not necessarily symmetrical arrangement, they provide the framework needed to bring out the floral detail, which might otherwise be lost in the exuberance of the planting.

Another way that box can be used for contrast is by taking advantage of its uniform, finely textured surface when clipped as a low hedge. When planted as a layer up against a taller hedge made from other green foliage, the contrast between the two is pleasing because the subtle difference in colour and texture produces a feeling of depth and complexity.

Hedges

Box is very suited for hedging in a contemporary garden where it is desired to create an informal effect. Hedges grown from beech, hawthorn or yew are cut with a straight, vertical surface, but the natural habit of box takes an undulating form and the fine texture of its foliage allows it to be trimmed to an irregular shape that looks pleasing to the eye and performs all the functions of a hedge. Informal box hedges need not take that long to achieve and they look perfectly presentable before they have achieved their final height.

An informal hedge in Kent borders a laid-out garden and a natural pond. This hedge has such an intrinsic character that it links harmoniously the structured garden on one side and an expanse of naturally wooded water on the other. The hedge is shaded by ancient oaks and strikes a perfect balance between two contrasting areas.

This box hedge in Herefordshire has been allowed to evolve over many years into its present majestic shape, which requires minimal annual shaping.

Box hedges do, in fact, have a way of evolving through different phases and successive generations of owners, so that their final form may be quite unlike the original. What may have begun as a straight-cut, regular hedge has a way of moving away from formality over many years through the design or, at times, neglect of their owners, to become wilder and more informal. Such a hedge is seen in a wonderful, natural garden in Herefordshire, which has reached a glorious state of maturity and defies any attempt to tame it in any way. It is a perfect complement to the garden that the owners have created.

The American Way

Boxwood, the name for box in America, was introduced to American gardens by the early colonists in the mid-seventeenth century with plants introduced from Europe. The famous Williamsburg gardens used box in a formal manner and they were similar to European designs of the time, although the use of topiary was restrained and the shaping of complex figures, such as bird and animal shapes, was not seen. Box has played a significant role in every style of garden since then, but the way in which it has come to be used in America is generally less formal and quite different to the European fashion. In America, box is generally allowed to maintain its natural growth form, rather than being clipped to a shape. Permitting the species and cultivars of *Buxus* to develop naturally produces a completely differently effect and, although this has been consistent in American design over the years, it feels a very contemporary way of using box on this side of the Atlantic at the present time. By adopting the American way of growing box and allowing it to thrive in its natural habit, we can bring a new and exciting informality to our garden design. If this approach is taken, it is important to choose the species or cultivar that has the habit that best suits the desired style of garden because there are enormous differences in the shape, colour and form of the various species and cultivars of the *Buxaceae*. (Details are given about some of these in Chapter 4.)

As with many projects involving box, time considerations will have a strong influence on what can be achieved and for this reason it is important to bear in mind the speed of growth when deciding which species or cultivar to plant. This will necessitate making

Unclipped boxwood in its natural form alongside a brick path in this informal setting at Dumbarton Oaks, Georgetown, Washington DC, USA. In the foreground is a Chinese quince tree.

difficult decisions at times because the box plants with the most sculptural shapes are also the ones that are slowest growing. This beautiful way of using box is not going to be the answer for many designers, but the natural forms of box and the subtle contrast between different varieties brings in a very natural (and low maintenance) character to the garden.

Box *per se*

While many gardeners are very happy to use box as one of their players, the occasional enthusiast is inspired to create a garden in which box topiary is the whole cast – and the chorus as well! One such gardener was inspired by visiting Séricourt in France and seeing how box topiary can fire the imagination. Séricourt is described as an allegorical garden where topiary is used to depict scenes from the nearby World War I battlefields and a visit can have a powerful effect. On returning to her beautiful garden at Old Place Farm, High Halden in Kent, Ann Eker brought together more than 350 pieces of box topiary that she arranged, with an exquisite sense of harmony, style and wit, around a path of stone paving in a corner of the garden. This topiary is planted in the mottled shade of *Betula pendula* birch trees and their silvery bark contrasts pleasingly with the deep green colour of the box. In sunlight, the shadows from its light foliage play across the topiary forms and the whole effect is restful and sublime. The box shapes, unlike at Séricourt, have no morbid associations; on the contrary, they create a feeling of enchantment and delight, with a sense of mystery about what some of the groupings might be taken to indicate: gatherings of villagers, barrows of warriors, a farmyard scene or even something out of the fairy imagination? Cones, spirals, balls and bird shapes of all sorts, including peacocks, are all present and the only man-made addition is a chair carved from a single tree. This garden is simply magical and leaves an abiding impression.

The magical box garden at High Halden, Kent. Hand-trimmed topiary specimens in many shapes and different sizes are arranged in a way that conjures up an enchanted atmosphere. The dappled shade of the birch trees and the contrasting colour of their silvery bark enhance the effect.

CHAPTER 3

BOX IN SMALL GARDENS

Creating a Special, Preserved Space

Creating a small garden presents different and often greater challenges than are faced when making plans for a larger area. Many of the blessings that gardens offer can be enjoyed in a small scale, but it is important to be quite clear about what you want to achieve before moving any earth or laying any flagstones, and it is important not to be too greedy, so that the overall effect is harmony, not clutter. Box is a useful tool in the designer's kit, particularly when thinking about the elements that will form the garden and putting the scheme together. There are hard features that may be already present, such as walls, fences, steps, a trellis or a garden building, and it is often desirable to add a natural element that will soften these hard necessities. In a small garden there may be no room for a tree or shrubs and in a confined space a natural element can be introduced with box. With its evergreen leaf and its ability to be trained into various shapes and forms, box is very adaptable and it will only require one clip a year. This plastic property of box can be used to reflect an object like a stone ornament, or to compose an entrance or a special area. Box can bring a unifying and calming framework to what might otherwise be a jumble, made up of too many components, too close together. A box hedge can be used to organize and unify these different areas and can be grown to a height that is compatible with the proportions of the design. The overall effect of a small garden should be to give the feeling of a special, preserved space. This is particularly the case when it is in an urban setting where the gardener will want to create an atmosphere that sets it apart from the bustle of the metropolitan surrounds. This requires the imagination to be put to work and it helps to adopt a somewhat theatrical approach.

Small gardens are inevitably limited by size, but it would not be helpful to be didactic about the exact dimensions intended. This chapter is more about how to make the most of an area where there is a limit to what can be included without compromising the overall effect by putting in more than the space allows. Box can help to achieve success in the overall design of a small garden, particularly by harmonizing and unifying the various elements, and by expressing and condensing an idea into a small area. The types of gardens where these ideas are most relevant will include urban gardens but also the domains within a larger garden where the same principles apply, such as a courtyard garden, a herb garden or a potager for growing vegetables.

Focal Points

A device used by designers, and particularly useful in a small garden, is the creation of a focal point that draws the eye toward it and increases the apparent space along the axis between the observer and the object, producing a sense of perspective. The focal point may be a sundial, a fountain or an elegant seat. To achieve the illusion of depth, it is essential that the sense of perception is deceived by having a series of visual cues along the axis as the focal point is approached. This can be achieved by having pairs of topiary figures, such as small box balls or cones, on either side. A focal point in a small town garden also has the important role of drawing the eye away from surrounding buildings and into the restful areas within the boundaries.

Paths

A great deal of thought will go into the planning of paths and paved or gravel areas in a small garden because, as well as being practical and functional, they are an essential part of the design and will define other elements. Box can reinforce the impact of paths in a small garden. When a path is straight and formal the addition of shaped and clipped box emphasizes

An urn on a plinth as a focal point at the end of a vista composed of a paved path leading on to grass, flanked by hedging and terracotta flower urns. The tall box tiers in the foreground strengthen the perspective.

the walkway and acts as a border for the beds, which contain the planting scheme. At a place where paths meet and link the different areas of the garden, clipped box at the intersection will give definition and add interest to what otherwise might be an unremarkable meeting of ways. If a narrow passage runs along the boundary of a town garden and there is not enough space or sufficient light to plant interesting shrubs and flowers along its length, a box hedge clipped to a narrow width will define the edge and give character to an otherwise unexciting pathway. One of the great strengths of box is that it will grow well in the shady areas of a small garden. A town garden will often be overshadowed by buildings and neighbouring trees, and a dark margin be redeemed by a border of box.

Functional Areas

A cutting garden is a great addition to a garden if there is space and if the layout of the land offers a suitable position. A special area designated for cutting flowers would fit comfortably in the business area of a garden, near the greenhouse, tool shed and the compost. It requires much the same conditions as a vegetable garden – an open aspect with full sun. It can be sur-

An unremarkable, shady passage leading from the front of the house to the garden, which has been given a lift by planting box hedging on both sides.

A cutting garden, sheltered by a garden wall, which is conveniently near the greenhouse and a water supply. The beds contain some perennials and are ready to be planted with annuals grown under glass.

This jam-packed potager provides the house with many of its needs, including cut flowers, vegetables and soft fruit, as well as apples. There is a forcing pot for rhubarb and, nearby, the greenhouse for bringing on seedlings. A neat box hedge contains this very busy area and integrates it with the small, stylish garden.

rounded by a low framework of box, which will set it apart from the rest of the area and adds to its ornamental nature. If the cutting garden is small, the choice of flowers should give as much seasonal value as possible. Access to the beds is important, and narrow paths will enable you to pick and manage the flowers, which will all be within easy reach. At the opening of these paths, and at intersections, the box hedge may be allowed to grow a little higher and it then can be clipped to form small decorative columns to mark the entrances. The margin of box hedging should be kept low and narrow, and a position with full sun is ideal. In subsequent years the box roots will need to be cut back a little from time to time with a small border spade or edging iron to prevent too much invasion

into the bed, with loss of nutrients from the cutting garden. For a keen flower-arranger, the planning and management of this productive area can give great pleasure.

Many small gardens will have some space to contain at least one area that can combine to serve several household functions. If the layout is given sufficient thought, a carefully chosen collection of espalier fruit trees, which are able to produce enough apple and pears for the household, a cutting garden with flowering plants for enjoying indoors and a potager for producing vegetables for the table, can all fit in. The advantage of enclosing special areas like these with a box hedge is that it makes an otherwise functional and potentially untidy part of the garden into one that has a style of its own that integrates with the rest of the garden in the overall design. The neatly clipped hedge that surrounds the potager makes sure that there is no overspill of the productive into the social area of the garden

Dedicated Spaces

In a large garden, the places that are set aside for a specific purpose can be spaced out and need not conflict. However, in a small garden this may not be an option. The idea of garden rooms has already been mentioned in Chapter 2 but they are a particularly useful feature when planning a small garden because of the need to fit more than one thing in to a limited area. An eating space with table and chairs, a sitting area or perhaps a water feature can be all be circumscribed with box hedges in order to give a feeling of separation, despite the limitation of space. Growing the box hedging into upright shapes at the entrance to the area creates an effect and marks out the special areas. It may be thought that separate garden com-

partments need to be in geometric shapes and, therefore, rather formal, but it is quite possible to use box in a flowing, contemporary fashion to define several different spaces with different ambiences.

Entrances and Openings

A narrow opening into an area within a small garden can give a pleasant sense of inquisitiveness of what may lie beyond. Here is an opportunity to increase the suspense by picking out the entrance with stylish pillars of box topiary or simple box balls, depending on the atmosphere you wish to create. The advantage of clipped hedging or topiary is that the specimens can be tailor-made to fit the area and they are clipped annually, so do not encroach on the opening. Punctuation of either side of an opening emphasizes its relevance and indicates that there is another part of the garden to explore. An opening may also lead to a change of level and box topiary placed on either side can usefully mark a potential hazard. Very often an entrance will require a gate, either for safety or for

Low box hedging demarcates separate rooms and links this part of the garden to the house by framing the steps. The ornamental pool and sitting area have four spirals to mark this out as a special area.

ABOVE: A decorative box hedge bordering a bed with *Tulipa* 'Maureen', hellebores and *Eleagnus* 'Quicksilver', leading to a picket gate.

LEFT: Two topiary cones standing on pedestals flank the doors of the garden entrance to the conservatory. The symmetry is emphasized by the masonry balls above.

privacy, and the style of the gate is likely to indicate what may lie beyond. A simple picket gate could open into a cottage garden, whereas a solid door adds an element of mystery.

Paved Areas

An area of hard landscaping positioned conveniently close to the house will be an accessible place for a table and chairs, and an easy place for entertaining. The severity of the rigid lines of brick or stone will be softened by adjacent planting and clipped box can take on the role of a go-between from the paved area

A seating area edged by the formality of yew topiary and box hedging, which contains a border.

to the softer shapes of the garden beyond, as its soft-structured growth complements the hard surfaces. In this transitional space, the box unifies the house and the garden. In a town garden there may only be room for a small area of paving, but space can be found within the paving, or at the edge, to incorporate cubes of clipped box, which can add definition to the whole area. This is a part of the garden where topiary combines well with hard landscaping and an interestingly clipped shape, such as a bird, can introduce another perspective to this social area by providing an element of drama. Gravel has a softer appearance than paving and topiary will thrive because there is no restriction to root growth nor to the availability of water and nutrients. Clipped shapes give opportunities for exciting contemporary design when they are chosen to define the mood of the garden.

Front of the House

It is surprising how infrequently box is planted in the front gardens of town houses where the space available and the lack of privacy make it unlikely that the area will be used as anything other than an approach to the front door. This clipped evergreen can introduce structure with a certain formality to an often neglected area and make it into an elegant eye-catcher, providing an opening gambit for conversation. The design can be very simple and a small geometrical shape using two colours of clipped box, *Buxus sempervirens* and *B. sempervirens* 'Elegantissima', will introduce composure to the approach to the front door.

In a rural situation, using box on either side of a central path will give a strong sense of design and bring composure to the layout of the front of the house, particularly if the planting is abundant, of the type that

The approach to this arts and crafts period house has a simple but effective knot design combining *Buxus sempervirens* and *B. sempervirens* 'Elegantissima'. The pale squares of the box complement the geometric pattern of the paving. This front garden is elegant and eye-catching and also very easy to maintain.

BELOW: Box balls combined with bergenias and perennial planting line the path to the front door of this village house.

would be found in a cottage garden. The juxtaposition of clipped shapes and free-flowing forms make an attractive combination.

In an urban situation, the contrast of a clipped mass of evergreen box is an antidote to the surrounding grey streets. If space is limited, a simple box design with some small shrubs or perennials will emphasize the way in to the house and give an unpretentious but strong addition to the front garden. If an edging is to be used around the design, then by choosing either local brick, a roofing tile or some other vernacular material, you will harmonize and add clarity to how the box design relates to the house. Another way to use box in a front garden is to complement a tree that is already in place with a surrounding circle of box. An intricate classical knot will probably not work in this position because it is over-complicated for the available space but, instead, plant a rope design of two colours of box twisted or braded together in an over and under design (*see* Chapter 2). A small run of steps that lead up to the front door can be planted either side with clipped box, which, as well as being pleasing to the eye, becomes a reassuring visual 'handrail' when stepping up or down. A considerable advantage of using box at the front of the house is that there will be minimal annual mainte-nance, giving more time to enjoy the private areas of your garden at the back of the house. Containerized

The entrance to a London house with a box design featuring a small rectangle and a central diamond. The colour of the evergreen leaves and the planting with lavender and roses make a contrast to the city street. The chequerboard-tile surround complements the geometric area of the front garden.

box topiary can be placed on either side of a front door and this makes an impact when the containers and the proportions of the topiary are in tune with the entrance. Putting box topiary in this important position has the great advantage that it will give form and interest throughout the year and, being evergreen and frost hardy, it will be a sustaining structure during the drab months in mid-winter.

Children's Garden

Box can be a delightful adventure area for the young. An early memory as a child is of playing in a box maze. The recollection of this magical domain with its pungent, aromatic scent of boxwood is still strong. The inclusion of an area that can be set aside for children in a large garden is simple to achieve, but doing this in a small garden will always be more difficult. The first step could be to dig some miniature beds for scattering seeds or perhaps constructing a small wooden playhouse. Either of these could be surrounded by a box hedge to mark out the space for their own dedicated area. Ownership of their own little garden can kindle an early interest in nature, where children can learn that water and warmth are necessary to germinate a dormant seed and that, once germinated, it needs

A child in a world of his own in a box scroll.

water and warmth in order to grow. At the Spring Garden Museum Plant Fair in London, box and topiary plants were on display and it was surprising how box plants fascinated young children; they were often drawn to small pieces of topiary, such as a bird or a mini lollipop. These small shapes aroused their interest and they would ask questions about how to begin making a shape and about how they should go about starting their topiary from a suitable plant. It may be that the balls and birds are everyday things that children find playful and can relate to and that they can imagine shaping such a plant on their own.

Topiary in Containers

Topiary grown in containers adds form and style to a small garden and can be used to bring interest to an awkward corner. A pot with a clipped ball or a spiral, or perhaps a dainty song-bird perched on top of a tier of clipped box, can become a focal point for a paved area where there is no opportunity to construct a border. Containerized topiary can be moved about the paving according to the season and treated rather like an installation at a museum. Where there is only space for a couple of chairs and a table outside the kitchen door, a small container of evergreen topiary can always be squeezed in to bring a little structure, or maybe just some amusement to the area, and a container of topiary can be the evergreen presence that converts a bare balcony into a miniature oasis of plants. A small box ball or cone is the popular choice for many city buildings that have a door that opens on to a terrace or balcony, where it is the dependable plant that gives pleasure throughout the year. (Care of plants in containers is covered in Chapter 5.)

An urn set in a yew circle planted with a box standard and annual planting, flanked by two square-topped box pillars.

A topiary figure of a stylized bird with a top-knot in a wooden container, sentinel to a doorway.

A box cone in a stone container set on a plinth surrounded by box. An otherwise quite plain, brick courtyard is brought to life by this feature.

Box is a perfect plant for a window box because it will look good at all times of the year and combines well with brightly coloured annuals. It also requires little maintenance and has the advantage of longevity. *Buxus sempervirens* is grown for this purpose and popular shapes, such as small balls and cones, are readily available. As an alternative to planting *B. sempervirens*, it is worth considering a slow-growing cultivar, such as *B. sempervirens* 'Suffruticosa' or *B. sempervirens* 'Justin Brouwers' as both have a compact and rounded habit and they will require very little attention. However, both 'Suffruticosa' and 'Justin Brouwers' are unlikely to be available as topiary and this is one of the times when growing your own plant is worthwhile.

Small Gardens in Winter

The aim, when designing a small garden, is to link the outside area to the house in such a way that they flow together and can be enjoyed from many perspectives

A small patio sitting area with climbing rose 'Gertude Jekyll' on a trellis and a group of topiary in clay pots, including a *Buxus sempervirens* 'Elegantissima' mini-standard with annual planting.

A window box with two box balls and summer planting.

in all seasons of the year. The views from inside the house are important – particularly in the winter when the garden is more likely to be seen from indoors. Box keeps its form and its colour, and you will find that the play of light on clipped shapes is very attractive on a bright wintery day. It is worth standing at the windows and imagining the view that you would like to frame with winter in mind, perhaps bringing in deciduous shrubs, such as dogwoods and viburnums with their distinctive bark and winter flowering, which make an attractive contribution to the border when everything else is dull. At that time of year, however, it is the evergreens that provide the strong shapes and give weight and definition to the vistas. During the winter months, a small garden will rely on the composition and bones of the garden. The effervescence of the colours of flowers and shrubs, which has been present during the summer, will no longer be present and the success of the garden will depend on the permanent structures and basic design. Within this framework, strong evergreen elements have an intrinsic value and will step into the limelight during the colourless winter months. Box topiary and hedging, which has been a main support to the exuberance of summer, will become the mainstay of winter. A fall of snow on the box is metaphorically (and sometimes literally) the icing on the cake!

A winter scene in the garden brought to life with a topiary plum-pudding surmounted by a generous topping of sauce.

CHAPTER 4

BOX SPECIES AND CULTIVARS

The Many Types of *Buxus*

Buxus is a genus of approximately 120 species in the family *Buxaceae*. In addition, there are about 350 cultivars, of which 150 are available commercially. These are listed and described in Lynn R. Batdorf's authoritative work, *Boxwood: An Illustrated Encyclopedia* (The American Boxwood Society, 2004). There are seven temperate *Buxus* species, but it is not always recognized that an even larger number of species are found in the tropical regions of the world. It is not my intention to give details of a great number of the species and cultivars, and only those used more commonly in garden design on account of their particular charm are featured.

Buxus sempervirens and some of its cultivars are often used by gardeners because they are suitable for topiary and hedging, but there are many other beautiful species and cultivars that are appreciated as free-growing plants and admired for their shape and colouring, despite the fact that they do not have the characteristics that make them suitable for clipping. Among the many types of *Buxus* there are enormous differences in the form of the leaves, as well as in the habit of growth. Species and cultivars can be found with colouring from blue-green to yellow-gold and variegated leaf colours that include both ends of this spectrum. Leaf shapes demonstrate a similar degree of diversity, with sizes and shapes varying greatly. Perhaps the largest contrast among the different *Buxaceae* is their habit. There is a cultivar of *Buxus* with the columnar shape of a Cyprus tree, while others have squat, mound-like forms. This is an extremely varied genus and the two notable features that draw them all together are their longevity and the fact that they are evergreen. If you decide to grow specimens of *Buxus* species and cultivars for their intrinsic beauty, it is wise to choose a position in the garden where there is no need to clip and constrain their shape, and where there is plenty of room to view them without being crowded, so that the plants can show their natural shape and structure. Position is also important because species and cultivars differ in their tolerance to certain conditions, and in their resistance to pests and disease. Some of the species and cultivars of *Buxus* that can be used and enjoyed as specimens in their own right are given below.

Buxus balearica

Buxus balearica is an attractive, densely branched plant with a regular habit that grows to 4.5–6m (14¾–19½ft) in height. It is native to the shores of the Mediterranean and vast forests were at one time present, particularly in Turkey and Spain. Sadly, the wood of *B. balearica*

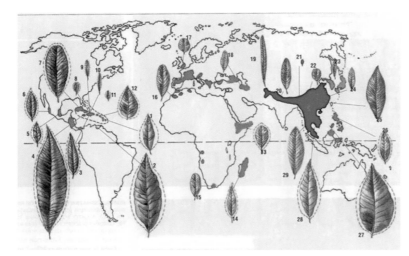

The distribution throughout the world of twenty-nine species of *Buxus*. The relative leaf size and shape of each of the species is shown.

BELOW: *Buxus balearica*. An attractive, dense tree with a regular habit. Forests of *B. balearica* were at one time seen across large areas of the countries bordering the Mediterranean, but its popularity for commercial use led to these being felled. Seen growing here at Sir Harold Hillier Gardens and Arboretum.

Key for Map Showing Geographical Distribution of 29 *Buxus* Species

1) *B. portoricensis*
2) *B. citrifolia*
3) *B. acuminata*
4) *B. macrophylla*
5) *B. mexicana*
6) *B. pubescens*
7) *B. crassifolia*
8) *B. rotundifolia*
9) *B. revoluta*
10) *B. foliosa*
11) *B. vaccinioides*
12) *B. cubana*
13) *B. hildebrandtii*
14) *B. madagascarica*
15) *B. macowani*
16) *B. balearica*
17) *B. sempervirens*
18) *B. hyrcana*
19) *B. papillosa*
20) *B. wallichiana*
21) *B. rugulosa* var. *prostrata*
22) *B. sinica* var. *sinica*
23) *B. harlandii*
24) *B. microphylla* var. aemulans
25) *B. megistophylla*
26) *B. rivularis*
27) *B. rolfei*
28) *B. cochinchinensis*
29) *B. rupicola*

gained a reputation for its commercial uses and these forests were cut down, leaving little left to be seen.

Buxus 'Green Velvet'

A broad, attractive cultivar with a loose habit.

Buxus harlandii

Buxus harlandii was first discovered growing at Tai tam tuk in Hong Kong by Dr Hance, a British botanist, in

Buxus 'Green Velvet' growing at Sir Harold Hillier Gardens and Arboretum, Hampshire.

1858. He brought it back to England and it became known as *B. harlandii* Hance. This is a beautiful species of box that has a dense habit with a multi-stemmed growth and an attractive bark with a distinctive low-growing, vase-shaped form, with leaves that are long and narrow and approximately 3.5cm (1½in) in length. There are many species and cultivars that can be successfully planted in groups, but this *Buxus* has such a wonderfully individual shape that it deserves to be planted as an individual specimen. *Buxus harlandii* is best cultivated in a sheltered position and may bronze if grown in strong sun or exposed to winter winds. A characteristic feature is that the top surface of the plant is flat, but this may simply be because it is one of the first species to produce growth, and this early growth can be affected by spring frosts, which may affect its shape in the long term.

Buxus 'John Baldwin'

A slow-growing *Buxus* with a broad, vertical habit and dense growth, which makes it resistant to breakage by

Buxus harlandii showing its typical vase-like shape, with some scarring to the top due to frost damage

heavy snowfall. In favourable conditions it will grow to 2.0 × 1.0m (6½ × 3¼ft) in twenty-five years. The leaves are relatively small, elliptical and fine-textured, and they have a bluish-green colour. Site conditions can affect the habit and colour of this plant; 'John Baldwin' grows best in a position with some shade. Because of its colour and attractive shape, 'John Baldwin' can be used as a specimen plant and it also makes a distinctive hedge that seldom needs tending.

Buxus microphylla 'Green Pillow'

A tightly branched plant with an extremely dwarf, mounded growth habit. The charm of 'Green Pillow' is its distinctive shape, which is appreciated when grown as a specimen plant, and it has been used as mass plantings in many prestigious sites. Horticultural consultant, Lynn Batdorf, reports that 385 'Green Pillow' were planted at 45cm (17½in) intervals in the Rose

ABOVE: Foliage of *Buxus harlandii* is long, narrow and shiny with a notched tip and prominent midrib.

Garden at the White House in the 1960s, and in 1996 he measured them and found that they were just 1m high and 1m wide. 'Green Pillow' has attractive green leaves all year and is not affected by frost.

Buxus microphylla var. *japonica* 'Faulkner'

A multi-stemmed shrub with an open, low and spreading habit. The leaves are thick with a waxy, deep green colour and a distinctive lustre, 2cm (1in) in length. It is able to keep its colour in all conditions, including winter, which makes it an attractive specimen plant. When grown as a specimen plant, 'Faulkner' should be positioned where there is plenty of space to allow its true structure to develop. To give an idea of its spread, a 'Faulkner' that I planted twenty-three years ago in my nursery in Kent is now 1.8m (6ft) wide

Buxus 'John Baldwin' with its broad habit and dense growth is a beautiful shape to grow as a specimen.

The natural, mounded shape of *Buxus microphylla* 'Green Pillow' growing at Sir Harold Hillier Gardens and Arboretum. This *Buxus* grows slowly and maintains its shape.

with a height of 1.1m (3½ft). This particular specimen of 'Faulkner' has never been pruned or affected by frost and grows in a chalk valley in good ground. 'Faulkner' is an example of a cultivar that should be grown for its own shape and not planted for clipped hedging or for topiary. In the past it was promoted in Europe as an alternative to *B. sempervirens* and propagated by growers because it was hoped that it might be more disease-resistant; there is some evidence that this is the case. However, 'Faulkner' has an open habit that is not conducive to close clipping and if a fine finish is required, then 'Faulkner' is not suitable for topiary and hedging

Buxus microphylla var. *japonica* 'National'

A shrub that grows vigorously, putting on a typical annual terminal growth of 13cm (5in). The leaves are glossy and deep green in colour. 'National' is said to thrive best in a light soil that drains well, particularly in winter. It grows relatively quickly to be a substantial, dense shrub that will be useful in a landscape setting.

Buxus 'Riparia'

A loose-formed box with attractive, oval-shaped leaves.

Buxus microphylla var. *japonica* 'Faulkner' showing its open growth and spreading habit. Note the attractive contrast between the deep colour of the mature leaves and the lighter spring growth.

BELOW: Deep-emerald leaves of *Buxus microphylla* var. *japonica* 'Faulkner' showing their characteristic waxy lustre.

BELOW RIGHT: *Buxus microphylla* var. *japonica* 'National'. A relatively fast-growing *Buxus* with a tall and wide habit that is useful for landscaping purposes, growing at Sir Harold Hillier Gardens and Arboretum.

Buxus 'Riparia' growing at Sir Harold Hillier Gardens and Arboretum.

Buxus sempervirens

Buxus sempervirens is the most widely used *Buxus* in garden design. It is known as common box in the British Isles and this nondescript title most certainly belies its fine history as a tree whose wood was used by the Phrygians, Egyptians, Greeks and Romans, and how great forests of *B. sempervirens* grew on the eastern shore of the Black Sea, the Caucasus Mountains and in the Elburz Mountains region of northern Iran. Plant explorers visiting Turkey in 1893 recorded finding a *B. sempervirens* forest east of Istanbul growing alongside yew, holly and fir. In those conditions the box had

grown to a height of 12m (39ft). Sadly, because of the popularity of boxwood for making musical instruments and other craft work, these forests have largely been harvested and no longer exist, apart from four or five large box forests in government-protected preserves (personal observation to the author from Lynn Batdorf who visited this area in 2002). *Buxus sempervirens* is the species that we primarily use for topiary and hedging because it perfectly fulfils that role and is proven to clip with an outstanding finish. The elements that are essential for topiary and hedging are the structure of the plant and the size of the leaf, as well as the annual rate of growth. This plant has a structure that is sufficiently open to allow air flow but also intricate enough to form the framework for a clipped specimen. *Buxus sempervirens* grows proportionally taller than wider, with an annual rate of growth in the region of 6–10cm (2–4in) and, importantly, its medium-sized leaf will clip neatly to a perfect finish. In many ways it is a victim of its own success because *B. sempervirens* is grown almost exclusively for topiary and hedging. When it is grown as a tree, its broad, conical habit and pale bark, which matures into a gnarled form, makes it very attractive.

Buxus sempervirens 'Aureo-Variegata'

This cultivar is known to have been in cultivation for more than 200 years and is sometimes referred to as 'golden box'. The leaves are variegated with green centres and yellow colouring to the margins. The mixture of colours in the variegation is diverse and the pattern on the leaves is not uniform. 'Aureo-Variegata' is able to grow in deep shade. If unchecked, it grows to be a large, rather disorganized shrub with a loose habit, yet dense enough to make a good addition to an informal large shrubbery or a screening border, where its light colouring adds relief to dark evergreens. An 'Aureo-Variegata' that I planted in my nursery in Kent twenty-four years ago now stands at 2.5m (8ft) with a width of 2.1m (7ft). Although its light colour makes a contrast to other *Buxus* types, 'Aureo-Variegata' is not suitable for creating patterns in knot designs because it has an insufficiently dense finish when clipped; this also makes it unsuitable for topiary.

Unclipped *Buxus sempervirens*, with a height of 1.75m (6ft) and 2.4m (8ft) width, growing beside a river. The roots are occasionally immersed, with no adverse effect to the plant.

Buxus sempervirens 'Blauer Heinz'

A very slow-growing *Buxus*, with a dwarf, dense habit and distinctive blue-green coloured leaves. The young leaves are particularly striking with an intense glaucous colour. Its habit and density are similar to 'Suffruticosa', which makes it suitable for clipping, and it has been planted in classic gardens for edging formal areas, although its slow rate of growth limits its use for most gardeners. The appearance of 'Blauer Heinz' with its pleasing spherical shape is very suitable as a specimen plant, particularly in spring with the intense colouring of the new leaves. 'Blauer Heinz' looks very elegant in a group and is all the better for being left unclipped. It is a recent cultivar, originating in 1972, and was named 'Blauer' for it blue-green foliage and Heinz after Heinz Grupe who worked for the great baroque garden of Herrenhausen in Hanover, Germany.

Buxus sempervirens 'Elegantissima'

'Elegantissima' has a light colouring that is the effect of variegated leaves with a creamy-white margin and a dark green centre. It grows slowly to be a shrub, approximately 2m (6½ft) high with a rounded and pyramidal

ABOVE LEFT: Shiny foliage of *Buxus sempervirens*.

The variegated *Buxus sempervirens* 'Aureo-Variegata' showing its loose habit.

habit. The variegation is generally stable but the odd branch may revert to green foliage. 'Elegantissima' is used in knot gardens and intricately designed parterres as a contrast to green-coloured *Buxus*, and has a very suitable structure for this use, as it has a tidy habit and clips well. 'Elegantissima' is successful when grown as small topiary, as it requires minimal clipping. It comes into its own on a winter's day with its beautiful bright variegation. It also has a role in a shady border where it can enliven an otherwise dull area of the garden. This cultivar also does well in a container because it only has an annual growth of 2–3cm (1–1½in) and has a less-active root system than *B. sempervirens*, requiring fewer nutrients and less re-potting. 'Elegantissima' has been grown commercially since the late-nineteenth century and is one of the most recognizable and successful of the variegated *Buxus*.

Buxus sempervirens 'Graham Blandy'

An unusual *Buxus* because of its columnar, fastigiate habit. A 25-year-old specimen that was 25cm (10in)

ABOVE: Variegated leaves of *Buxus sempervirens* 'Aureo-Variegata' with green centres and yellow colouring to the margins.

Buxus sempervirens 'Blauer Heinz' showing its typical spherical habit. This specimen has never been clipped.

Bluish-green foliage of *Buxus sempervirens* 'Blauer Heinz' with a matt, rather than a lustrous, surface.

BELOW LEFT: *Buxus sempervirens* 'Elegantissima' standing out in a mixed border of shrubs and trees with *B. sempervirens* on the right

BELOW RIGHT: Variegated leaves of *Buxus sempervirens* 'Elegantissima'. The light colouring and interesting variegated detail make them very suitable as miniature table arrangements at Christmas time.

high when it was planted in my nursery in Kent is now 3.8m (12½ft) tall with a width of 40cm (16in). The plant is growing in a north-facing part of the garden, under trees with protection from the wind and it has required virtually no pruning. Ideally, this spectacular *Buxus* should be grown in shade because plants grown in full sun tend to open up as the columnar growth matures and pruning is required to maintain the distinctive and very beautiful, Cyprus-like form. The growth rate of the specimen of 'Graham Blandy' grown in Kent is 15cm (6in) annually. Therefore, for a *Buxus* cultivar, 'Graham Blandy' grows quickly and it is a plant that has a considerable potential to be used as a specimen, whether standing as a column in glorious isolation or in a group to strengthen an area or situated in a border for contrast. Another cultivar that grows in a columnar form and does not need clipping is *Buxus sempervirens* 'Dee Runk'.

A specimen of *Buxus sempervirens* 'Graham Blandy' 3.8m (12.5ft) tall, which has maintained its tight, columnar form without any clipping.

Buxus sempervirens 'Dee Runk' growing in a garden in Washington, USA. Although tall, it is not as elegantly columnar as 'Graham Blandy'.

Buxus sempervirens 'Handsworthiensis'

'Handsworthiensis' is a good choice for a gardener who is looking for a strong-growing *Buxus* for screening a boundary or landscaping a border in the garden, including a shady one. Its habit is ideal for this purpose as it is a large, upright and bushy shrub with attractive dark-green glossy leaves. It has the advantage of an annual growth of 10–15cm (4–6in) and a specimen that I have been growing for more than twenty years at my nursery measures 3.5m (11½ft) high and 1.8m (6ft) wide. 'Handsworthiensis' can be enjoyed in the winter months, making a striking lush evergreen contribution to the garden. Although cut box is long-lasting in water, florists would not normally include it in their list of evergreens for arranging in their displays. However, this box is a wonderful evergreen for flower arrangements as stems can be judiciously cut from a mature plant without damaging its shape and the stems are stiff, giving the arrangement structure.

Buxus sempervirens 'Justin Brouwers'

A slow-growing plant with dense growth and a mounding habit. 'Justin Brouwers' matures into a wonderfully natural cloud-like shape that has been used by many contemporary garden designers. If planted in a group, 'Justin Brouwers' will in time merge to make complementing, billowing, organic shapes. I planted a specimen of 'Justin Brouwers' in a position with some sun and dappled shade at my nursery in Kent twenty-four years ago and this now measures 1m (3ft) high and 1.15m (4ft) wide. This box is among the cultivars that are more susceptible to box blight.

Buxus sempervirens 'Latifolia Maculata'

A compact, dense plant that grows into a spreading form when mature. The leaves are dark green and irregularly variegated with streaks and splashes of yellow, which makes them an attractive feature of knot designs when used as a contrast to darker forms of *Buxus*. It has attractive, bright-yellow spring foliage, which is more intense when grown in a sunny situation. When it is clipped annually, 'Latifolia Maculata' can be grown as a dense,

A *Buxus sempervirens* 'Handsworthiensis' tree 3.5m (12ft) high, growing in a shaded position. The mature growth is deep-green and there is an annual growth of 10–15cm (4–6in).

Natural billowy growth of *Buxus sempervirens* 'Justin Brouwers'.

A 22-year-old specimen of *Buxus sempervirens* 'Latifolia Maculata' growing in a mixed border has a height of 2.3m (7½ft).

ABOVE: Leaves of *Buxus sempervirens* 'Latifolia Maculata' with irregular variegation.

low hedge and it is also a valuable addition to a mixed shrub border, where its unclipped form will merge with other shrubs and form a natural boundary.

Buxus sempervirens 'Myosotidifolia'

A slow-growing shrub with small, narrow, glaucous leaves. 'Myositidifolia' is a particularly pretty dwarf *Buxus* with a compact, oval habit. It has the rather intriguing common name of 'forget-me-not-leaf box-wood' and it is certainly very different to any of the other box covered in this section because of the appearance of its leaves. Although this *Buxus* was discovered in Europe more than 100 years ago, it is rarely grown in either North America or the British Isles; it would be good to see it more widely used.

Buxus sempervirens 'Myosotidifolia' with its compact, oval shape. An unclipped specimen.

Buxus sempervirens
'Newport Blue'

'Newport Blue' generally grows from four upright trunks that come from the main trunk near the ground and this produces a plant with parallel sides and a pyramidal top. Young leaves are lighter with a bluish tinge and the mature leaves dark in colour and shiny.

Buxus sempervirens
'Pendula Parasol'

Named in recognition of its broad, overhanging canopy, which throws shade like a parasol. 'Pendula Parasol' is an attractive specimen tree with its loose form and unusual habit.

ABOVE: Short (12mm) and narrow (4mm) leaves of *Buxus sempervirens* 'Myosotidifolia'.

Buxus sempervirens 'Newport Blue' growing at Sir Harold Hillier Gardens and Arboretum. Tall, broad tree with dark-green leaves.

Buxus sempervirens 'Pendula Parasol' has a distinctive pendulous habit and makes an attractive specimen, growing at Sir Harold Hillier Gardens and Arboretum.

Buxus sempervirens 'Suffruticosa'

'Suffruticosa' is a cultivar that has traditionally been used for low edging and for parterres and knot gardens, but its natural rounded shape makes it ideal for growing as a small specimen. This box cultivar is known as dwarf box, although if allowed to grow it would reach a height of 3–4m (9¾–12¾ft), at an annual rate of growth of only 2–3cm (¾–1¼in) a year. Its habit is dense with multiple branches and will naturally form a rounded shape. If you decide to use 'Suffruticosa' in a knot design, it is important to space

Buxus sempervirens 'Suffruticosa' growing unclipped. Note the dense foliage and the naturally rounded shape.

Buxus sinica var. *insularis* 'Tide Hill' showing its low, spreading growth. The branches root in the ground and it can be used as ground cover but only progresses by 3.5–4cm (1–1½in) per year.

BELOW: Small (15–25mm), shiny leaves of *Buxus sempervirens* 'Suffruticosa'. Note the small notches at the tips of the leaves.

the small plants further apart than normally advised, planting at a healthy 25cm (10in) or more. This will mean that the pattern will take longer to mature, but resisting the urge to plant tightly together will reduce the risk of fungal disease, which is drawn to damp, crowded conditions. If, in time, the 'Suffruticosa' hedging becomes too dense, it is advisable to thin out the plants by pruning deep into each plant in order to maintain a healthy, free circulation of air. Because the 'Suffruticosa' cultivar is neatly rounded and slow-growing, it is the perfect *Buxus* to use in window boxes, as its natural round habit and dense foliage will require minimal clipping and the roots also remain compact in the restricted space of a container. 'Suffruticosa' can also be trained into tiny, standard lollypops for planting in raised containers.

Buxus sinica var. *insularis* 'Tide Hill'

'Tide Hill' is included because of its rather unique property as a low-growing and spreading dwarf shrub with an attractive dense canopy and slow growth. This property as ground cover can be useful to the gardener but eventually, in say twenty to thirty years, 'Tide Hill' tends to outlast its usefulness by developing a disorganized and prostrate shape with the tendency for branches to root in the ground and for the centre to die back. This cultivar was named in 1954 in New Jersey, USA.

CHAPTER 5

PLANTING AND PROPAGATING BOX

A satisfaction of planting box is the knowledge that this long-lived genus will, with good care, be there for many years to come. In the way that we would diligently choose the right position and prepare the ground for planting a tree, we should do the same for box and set out to improve the site to ensure the longevity of the plant. To do this it is important to have suitable conditions and to identify any potential problems.

Choosing and Preparing the Site

Light Conditions

Box is versatile and can be relied on to grow well in most places and, although the effects of sun and shade do influence its growth, box thrives in sunny, open conditions as well as in shade. In smaller gardens, where there is less choice when choosing the site, it is advisable to avoid areas with a mass of overhanging trees and heavy shade or to take measures to lighten the cover, particularly if planning a knot or a parterre. Unclipped box can be planted as part of an informal screen or in a mixed shrubbery and will thrive in a shady area at the boundary of the garden. There are box species and cultivars that grow well in these situations (*see* Chapter 4) and will be unaffected by less light, particularly as they are unlikely to be clipped. There is an inevitable problem when planting in a bed that is close to a house or wall because eventually the shaded side of the topiary will become thin and lack good growth. For this reason, a focal piece of topiary should be given enough space and light to allow it to grow well on all sides. A solution for a containerized plant placed against the side of a building is to swivel the pot periodically to allow the weaker side to recover. When a low edging of box is planted tight against a wall there may be die-back after some time, which will require remedial pruning of some dead branches. This will improve the growth of the plants by increasing light and air circulation and encourage rejuvenation.

Drainage

A vital consideration when choosing the ground is to assess how well it drains, because box will not thrive in water-logged soil. This problem could occur because the ground is compacted. In a recently constructed garden this may be the result of disturbance and heavy machinery; if this is the case, soil improvement is required. However, if the ground is prone to being wet and all the signs of poor drainage exist, the solution is to lay land drains and these will deal with the issue so long as the water can flow to a lower level, such as a ditch, stream or soakaway. Perforated plastic pipes should be laid in trenches and when dealing with a sizeable area it is advisable to involve a landscape or specialist contractor who is skilled in designing and installing a drainage system.

Clearing the Ground

Clearing the planting area is best carried out over a few months. Prepare the ground well in advance by removing the annual weeds and clear the deep-rooted perennials, which often re-grow despite the best attempts to eliminate them. Thorough elimination of persistent weeds, such as bindweed and ground elder, is essential at this stage because it will be more difficult to do so after planting. The last resort is to use a glyphosate spray in order to target the remaining tough perennials. If a systemic control is necessary, the advice is that usage should be minimal and that the manufacturer's instructions are followed. When the proposed site is a lawn, the turf can be dealt with by lifting with a spade and putting elsewhere in the garden to rot down, as it will, in due course, become good loamy soil. For a larger expanse of lawn, it is advisable to use a self-propelled turf cutter, which will lift the sods efficiently and leave a clear area ready for the next stage.

Identifying the Soil Type

The pH will affect the availability of essential nutrients and the optimum soil pH for box is between 6.8 and 7.5. You may wish to test the soil but it is possible to have a good idea of your pH by looking at the natural vegetation and identifying which plants are growing well in your environment. If the soil test shows a reading below 6.5, the addition of dolomitic lime is appropriate; this is discussed further in Chapter 7.

Quality of the Soil

Box topiary and hedging will benefit from assiduous preparation in order to ensure longevity and good growth. All soils can be improved by working in organic matter and this is particularly true of clay and sandy soils. Clay soil will often lack good drainage in the winter and become solid and unworkable in the summer, while sandy soils have a tendency to leach nutrients and water. For these reasons, both of these types of soils will benefit from large quantities of rotted manure or garden compost. Mushroom compost, being alkaline, is useful for sandy soils, which tend to be acidic. Digging bulky organic matter into the ground improves the texture and structure of the soil when it breaks down and facilitates nutrient release. This is particularly true for severely compacted ground because drainage and the air content are restricted. When the ground has not previously been worked on, it will be necessary to dig over the area to relieve the compaction and break up any lumps of clay and remove larger stones and debris. It is an easier matter when the ground has been previously cultivated, as forking over will be sufficient to prepare for adding the organic matter. Lay 5cm (2in) of the organic material over the surface of the ground and gradually work it into the soil to about the depth of a spade. Allow the ground to settle before moving to the next stage, which is to rake the surface in order to produce a fine tilth.

Choosing and Nurturing Suitable Box Plants

It is not always easy to navigate your way through the wholesale and retail market when buying plants. The big growers of box are in Northern Europe and they have a highly efficient way of reaching their market, which would normally involve a local retailer who will supply appropriate plants and give advice. The system works as long as the plants are handled well at every stage.

Traditionally, the time to plant box is between November and March; this is certainly the only period for planting bare-rooted or root-balled plants. The term 'bare-rooted' refers to a plant that has been lifted from the ground and sold without soil; only small plants are suitable for this method of transplanting. Costs are lower for bare-rooted and root-balled plants, so when possible take advantage of the dormant season, as this can make a vast difference to the price for a large project, such as a parterre or knot garden. Difficulties can arise if there is poor handling of the plants from the time that they are lifted and dispatched by the grower to the time they reach the customer. The recipient should plant them into well-prepared ground at the earliest opportunity and avoid the worst of the winter weather. Inevitably, the bare-rooted plant will have root disturbance and once re-planted there will be a period before the roots become fully functional. The plant is unlikely to produce much new growth during the first year and leaf development may be paler in colour. Normal growth will return in the following spring. Resist clipping bare-rooted box in the first year after planting in order to allow all the plant's energy to go toward establishing good roots. Sometimes young hedging plants have strong leaders and these should be pruned back with secateurs to the level of the over-all height of the hedge. During its first and second years in the ground, bare-rooted hedging should be carefully monitored and watered whenever necessary.

The term 'root-balled' is used when a plant is lifted with the soil around the root intact and protected with hessian sacking. This method is used when lifting and selling larger specimens of either topiary or unshaped hedging plants. The intact root-ball gives the plant some protection between lifting and planting, but in the same way as for the bare-rooted plant, careful handling is required and the root-ball must be kept frost-free, not allowed to dry out and planted at the earliest opportunity. If it is necessary to wait for opti-mum planting conditions, box can be stored in a sheltered place or in an unheated building away from a drying wind or frost. When deciding on whether the hessian should be removed or not, use common sense. If the hessian wrapping can be untied without disturb-ing the root-ball, then take away the cloth, but leave it intact if the ball appears crumbly and fragile. If left, the sacking will eventually biodegrade, but that will take time and may hinder the emerging roots.

Containerized box plants can be bought and planted at any time of the year. They have the advan-tage that there will be no root disturbance and will, therefore, quickly establish themselves in the ground. However, it is worth examining before buying because if they are root-bound, they will be deficient of ferti-lizer and nutrients, and this will affect their progress at an early stage.

Watering newly planted box is easy to overlook and it is the one measure that must be attended to assidu-ously throughout the first two years. Keep a watchful eye on the moisture content of the ground from early spring to early winter and water whenever necessary,

ensuring that the soil never dries out. However, care should be taken not to over-water because water-logged ground will cause root rot by reducing the available oxygen.

Planting Box

Planting a Bare-Rooted Box Hedge

Preparing the ground for a low-growing box hedge should be as thorough as the preparation for planting large items of topiary. Young box plants that have been lifted during the dormant season by a commercial grower will be sold bare-rooted, with abundant roots of approximately 15–20cm (6–8in) in length. These roots must not dry out before planting and any damage should be pruned with secateurs. When planting a length of box, it is important to improve the soil all around the roots and a small planting hole should be avoided. Prepare a trench, which will permit the roots to drop perpendicularly and spread out horizontally, so that when backfilling, the topsoil will distribute between the fine roots and eliminate potential air pockets. Sprinkle bonemeal evenly over the dug-out soil and mix in well before planting. This will gradually break down and provide the phosphorus required to establish strong roots. Once planted, heal around each plant and gently firm the ground to ensure that the first flare of roots is level with the soil surface. Avoid plant-ing too deeply or over-compacting the ground. Expect the roots to take time to establish; it is vital that the plants are watered after planting and during the year until the late autumn, and again in the growing season of the following year.

Transplanting

Sometimes it is necessary to transplant a large box shrub or a specimen of topiary. The structure of the surface roots of *Buxus* makes this a completely viable procedure, but moving a large and established speci-men requires planning and preparation. It is best to lift either in the early autumn or early spring. October is a reliable month because the cooler days combined with the relatively warm soil help the roots to settle into the new planting position and establish them-selves before the weather turns foul. Early spring is also a safe time to transplant, but the timing is crucial because this must be done after the worst of the winter weather and before the signs of developing young growth. When planning to move a particularly large and established specimen, it is advisable to involve a specialist who will prepare by carrying out a programme of root pruning in order to encourage young fibrous roots that are sufficiently developed and are able to mitigate the upheaval of replanting.

Preparing the Planting Hole

The first stage is to prepare the planting hole, which should be generously wide and only as deep as the transplanted root-ball. If a specimen is being moved within the garden, the width of the root ball will be indicated by measuring the plant's drip line before excavation. This is done by etching a circle in the clean ground around the area defined by the outer circumference where water drops from the leaves to the ground. Begin by digging down one spade depth around the etched line to give guidance for the width of the prepared planting hole. To check the hole for good drainage, fill it with water prior to planting and if the water fails to drain, this will indicate a problem that will necessitate breaking up the subsoil and improving the structure of the soil at the base of the hole

A trench is dug around the box tree before transplanting. The width of the trench needs to be sufficiently wide to ease the root ball out by rocking to and fro.

The prepared root ball with a surrounding trench. The root ball is ready to be lifted after it has been wrapped in hessian cloth to preserve its structure.

Lifting the Plant

When lifting, the root ball must be firm and compact, so before any digging begins, ensure that the ground is neither too wet nor too dry. If the soil is too dry, it will crumble and fail to form a satisfactory root ball; if too wet, it will be very difficult to work. Box roots do not grow deeply but spread out widely and the outer root hairs should be included in the root ball. In preparation, brush away any fallen leaves and debris from the surface under and around the plant. Next, dig a clear-cut trench outside the circumference, then dig deeper and gradually undercut the ball at an angle of 45 degrees. At this point there will be roots appearing around the surface of the ball, which should be cut and tidied with sharp loppers and the surface of the ball should be smoothed by removing the excess soil. Once it is certain that the root ball is well established, wrap it with a sheet of hessian by tipping the ball one way and then another, easing it under and around until it protects the ball.

Re-Planting

Fit a lifting sling strap securely around the ball in preparation for a mechanical lift from the hole to the new planting position. At this stage, it would be reassuring to measure the root ball and check that the new planting position has the correct dimensions. Lower the transplanted box into the planting hole and remove the straps and hessian covering. Gradually backfill the hole with top soil, with the addition of bonemeal and a compound of mycorrhizal fungi, and thoroughly firm the ground to avoid air pockets. Water after planting and continue to do so from early spring to late autumn, and for the following two years during the growing season.

Planting a Box Tree

Box is hardly ever planted with the intention of allowing it to grow to its full size and this is regrettable because a mature box tree is magnificent and a grove of box trees even more so. Part of the reason for this is that *Buxus sempervirens* clips so well and is invariably grown for this primary purpose, for which it is so well suited. It is not sufficiently recognized that in time box trees can grow to over 7.5m (30ft). In the same way that the trunk of a mature olive tree will impress with its striking appearance, box grows slowly and develops a beautiful shape and enormous character with increasing age. If you can find a place in your garden where a box tree

The transplanted box tree has been moved to its new site.

might develop into a majestic specimen over the course of many decades, there is a strong argument to do this for the benefit of succeeding generations.

Planting Box in Containers

Container-grown topiary has an important role to play in the paved areas of a garden and where there is no opportunity to plant. Its ornamental qualities will frame an entrance or walkway and generate an atmosphere wherever it is used. Containerized box topiary will grow well and remain healthy, so long as sufficient attention has been given to choosing a suitable pot that gives the roots space to grow. It also needs to be

planted with a well-balanced compost and a slow-release fertilizer, and must be watered from April to October. However, after many years, even if all the rules have been followed, containerized box topiary will lose some strength and lack the bushiness of an equivalent specimen that has been grown in the ground. At this point, the topiary may benefit from being transferred to the ground in order to regain its vigour.

The Container

One reason why box grows well in containers is on account of the fact that it is not deep-rooted; therefore, the most suitable containers are wide and

A very old box tree growing next to St Martin's Church in Dorking. Dorking is near Box Hill, the site of an ancient box woodland situated on steep, west-facing chalk slopes in Surrey.

Topiary spirals and cones have been brought in to add to the splendour of a special occasion.

relatively shallow. Choose a container that is a little larger than the root-ball, allowing room for the roots to develop, but not so deep that it will require a mass of compost under the root ball, which will become water-logged and drown the roots, leading to root rot and disease.

Compost with Slow-Release Fertilizer

The roots will require sufficient compost around the root ball for new roots to form and grow into the pot. The compost should be an open material containing some loam and a coarse material, such as perlite, grit or vermiculite, to give good aeration and drainage, with the addition of a balanced, controlled, slow-released fertilizer with trace elements. Alternatively, this mixture of sterile loam with a balanced growing medium and nutrients can be purchased as a prepared formula, available as John Innes 3. The nutrients will be sufficient for one to two months of growing to give the plant a start. However, it is beneficial to add a controlled-release fertilizer to all composts as the granules have been developed to be present and active during the entire growing season.

The Roots

The plant should be top-dressed annually with a controlled slow-release fertilizer, but after two or three years there may be some indication of stress, which is often shown by loss of colour and leaf-fall caused by the lack of nutrients. This may be because the roots have become 'pot bound', which can be confirmed by removing the topiary from the pot. If a dense matt of roots has formed around the root ball on the inside of the container, they no longer have space for further growth. At this stage, the plant will either need to be re-potted into a larger container or kept in the same-sized pot after pruning the roots. Lifting out a small root ball for re-potting or root pruning is straightforward, but it can be difficult to pull out a large pot-bound topiary because of its weight and the tightness of the roots. This job can be made easier by placing the container on its side and easing the root ball from side to side and away from the pot. An additional method for removing a large and particularly stubborn root ball from its container is to use a *Root Assassin* shovel. This tool has double-edged serrated sharp teeth and can be used to slice the roots away from the inside of the container, making it possible to ease the topiary from its pot.

Re-Potting into a Larger Container

Once the roots have been removed from the container, prise and tease out the tight mesh of congested roots and, with a sharp pair of secateurs, trim back any straggly ends. Choose a slightly larger container that will allow a generous amount of fresh compost and fertilizer around the root ball. The ideal time of year to repot is in early spring; however, if the plant is in a weak and distressed state, it is best to deal with the roots immediately, whatever the time of year, and to water assiduously throughout the growing season. Mix your fresh compost, ideally a John Innes 3 loam mixture. The nutrients contained will not be active after two months, and it will then be beneficial to add controlled slow-release fertilizer granules. Repot the topiary, ensuring that the top of the root ball sits comfortably below the rim of the pot and that the surface roots are not deeply buried. Check that the topiary is well positioned in the pot and if there is a central stem, be sure that it is perpendicular. Finally, the compost should be firmed to eliminate any air pockets and watered until it emerges from the drainage holes.

Root Pruning in Order to Repot into the Same Container

The purpose of root pruning is to cut away enough of the congested root ball so that the topiary can be re-potted back into its original container. The method is to lay the plant on a firm surface and, with a sharp knife, firmly slice off equal sections of the thickened roots. Use a hand fork or pronged cultivar and tease out the inner cut roots and replant into a compost mixed with a controlled slow-release fertilizer.

Watering of Topiary in Containers

Regular watering of all plants in containers is essential throughout spring and summer up until late autumn, particularly during high temperatures. Water the pot until you see small droplets draining from the base. Unlike many plants, box will not show the early signs of lack of water and when it does, some damage will have been done. The first sign is when the young shoots become glaucous in colour (*see* Chapter 7). Another sign is that the leaves become papery to touch and pale in colour. Beware of the misconception that a few showers of rain will do the job for you. This is not the case because box foliage is dense and does not allow rain to penetrate into the pot. Unfortunately, once the

ABOVE LEFT: A pot-bound plant that requires root pruning so that young, emerging roots are in contact with the compost.

ABOVE RIGHT: Sufficient congested roots have been removed and the plant is ready to be re-potted into the same 5ltr container with compost and a controlled slow-released fertilizer.

roots have been left dry over a period, there is no way back and sad examples of this can often be seen in towns outside a shop or restaurant where the staff's attention has been elsewhere

Replenishing Nutrients for Plants Grown in Containers

Plants grown in containers have particular needs because frequent watering washes out nutrients and these are not renewed, as they would be with plants growing in soil. This leads to deficiencies of minerals, the signs of which should be looked out for. When the plant becomes generally pale in colour with yel-lowing of the lower leaves, this may indicate nitrogen deficiency and the compost requires a spring dress-ing of fertilizer. A further sign of element deficiency is discolouration of the border and tip of the leaves. A sign of magnesium deficiency is an orange/yellow tip to the leaves. Another frequently occurring deficiency shows itself by a creamy yellowing along the margin and tip of the leaf and this points to lack of phospho-rus. Whereas the use of synthetic fertilizers containing inorganic chemicals and trace elements is not necessary for plants grown in soil, these preparations do have a place in maintaining the health of box in containers.

Box is a resilient plant but the minimum amount of routine care is necessary because the signs of dehydration are not apparent until too late. These poor balls are obviously long gone.

BELOW LEFT: Magnesium deficiency with orange/yellow tips to the leaves.

BELOW: Phosphorus deficiency with creamy yellow tips to the leaves.

Propagation

Most people will buy their plants from nurseries or garden centres and do not have the inclination to produce their own. However, the gardener who is prepared to plan ahead and wait for the results will find it enormously rewarding to propagate their own box plants from cuttings. Propagation is surprisingly easy and extremely enjoyable, so long as there is the time and the available space. The chief deterrent is the delay before propagated plants can be put out in the garden – it will take three years from taking a cutting to achieving a small, well-branched and bushy plant. One advantage of propagating your own plants is the cost and another advantage is the certainty of producing healthy plants. Some of the species and cultivars of *Buxus* will root more successfully than others. For instance, it is possible to achieve a near 100 per cent success rate with *Buxus sempervirens* cuttings, whereas *B. sempervirens* 'Elegantissima' will not be as successful.

Propagation is almost invariably achieved by taking cuttings, but two other methods should be mentioned, if only to be dismissed. Propagation by seed is serendipitous because it relies on a plant producing flowers and this does not often occur in box reared in the usual conditions in a garden where it is regularly clipped. Flowers are seen on naturally growing plants, particularly those under stress, but the fine seeds are difficult to collect. Layering is another method of propagating new plants. A lower stem is buried in the ground where it produces roots while still attached to the parent. Layering is an excellent way to produce a limited quantity from a particular specimen, but it is not effective for producing a larger number of plants if your plan is to use them for a hedge or border. Plants produced by layering or cutting will be identical to the parent plant, while seedlings will grow into slightly different forms to the parent.

How to Take a Box Cutting

Hygiene is important and it is good practice to ensure that secateurs and knives are kept sharp and sanitized. Choose your material from a bush that is pest-free and cut from growth that is one or two years old, avoiding mature branches. Select robust growth and pick stems that have approximately 5cm (2in) of ripened wood at the base. A good cutting will be in the region of 8–12cm (3–5in) long with side shoots because this will produce a bushy plant from the outset. However, when you plan to produce shapes of topiary that require height, such as cones or spirals, single stems work in your favour. Conversely, when setting out to grow topiary balls, begin with a small multi-stem cutting because it is better to balance the width with the height. Ideally, when the cuttings are being collected for a hedge, knot garden or parterre, the cuttings should be as uniform as

possible. The cuttings can be taken from August to late October, preferably early in the morning if the weather is hot. Take the cuttings with a sharp pair of secateurs and avoid wilting by keeping them covered as you work and collect them in a plastic bag. Some cuttings can also be taken with a 'heel', which you do by carefully pulling away a suitable side shoot from its mature base without tearing the parent plant. Trim the heel to avoid infection. This is an excellent way of taking a cutting because the tissue in the heel contains the growth hormone auxin, which helps to promote rooting. When taking box cuttings, it is best to work in manageable batches so that the material can be planted into the prepared compost as speedily as possible.

Cuttings taken in September, which are ready to be set in a container with an equal mixture of compost and perlite or grit.

A cutting showing a heel where it was taken from the stem. The advantage of the heel is that it contains hormones that promote growth.

Preparing a Mix of Cutting Compost

The material used for growing cuttings should ideally contain equal portions of a peat-free compost and either grit or perlite, because it is important that the mixture has an open structure with easy drainage. The advantages of propagating in containers, rather than setting the cuttings straight into a prepared nursery bed, are that the moisture content can be managed, weed and climate can be controlled and disturbance from animals avoided. The choice of container depends on the quantity of cuttings to be taken. For just a few cuttings a small pot will work well, but for a larger number, a plastic window box is very effective. The depth of the container should be no more than 15–20cm (6–8in) and it is important to have good drainage holes. Water

generously to ensure that the whole mixture is damp and firm the compost before putting in your cuttings. It is advisable to reduce the bacteria count by using mains water rather than stored rainwater.

Preparing and Setting the Cuttings

Remove the leaves and any lateral growth from the bottom half of the cutting and insert into your pot. With certain species and cultivars, the cutting is delicate and it is necessary to use a pencil-thin spike to make the hole for the cutting. Common box, *Buxus sempervirens*, is more sturdy and can be inserted without the spiking procedure. The cuttings should be set in the container without overcrowding to ensure that there is some airflow. It is not necessary to cover box cuttings with glass or polythene during the lengthy period that it takes to develop the roots. Rooting hormone is applied to some types of semi-ripe cuttings, but trials have shown that it does not speed the rooting process significantly for box.

Positioning the Containers

The cuttings will remain in their containers for approximately nine months and it is essential to place them in a shady, north-facing position where they can be easily monitored to ensure that they receive adequate moisture and warmth. The cutting containers should be left undisturbed until the following summer when it is time to inspect the root development. The way to decide whether cuttings have rooted is to gently tug the stems and if there is resistance, it indicates that there are well-developed roots. Some cuttings will develop faster than others and it is advisable to wait until the majority have developed a viable root system, at which point it will be time to bring them on until they are robust enough to be planted out in the garden. The choice is to plant out into a nursery bed or to put them into small pots. Pots have the advantage of providing a controlled environment to manage the amount of water, the elimination of weeds and a balance of nutrients by using a long-acting, slow-release fertilizer. The disadvantage is the cost of purchasing pots and of nutrient, the close management of watering and the need to pot on annually until the plant reaches the required size for planting in the garden. Managing the plants in a nursery bed has the advantage of low cost but there is the effort of cultivating the bed, weed control and the management of nutrients.

These cuttings were lifted in July, having been put in containers the previous September. They show good root development.

BELOW: These *Buxus sempervirens* three-year-old plants in containers are ready for planting.

CHAPTER 6

MAKING TOPIARY SHAPES

Living Sculpture

Art and the garden come together when creating a new piece of topiary. Topiary is a fascinating form of sculpture because, unlike when creating a figure from a chunk of wood or a lump of clay, the nurture of living material is central to the success of a topiary shape, and alongside the training of the plant, the overriding objective is to maintain its good health. For anyone venturing into topiary design it is intriguing to remember that the gardeners at Pliny the Younger's villa at Laurentum were doing exactly the same thing in Italy 2,000 years ago and that the creativity of today's gardener is part of this long-lived tradition.

Some of the most successful designs of topiary are simple and uncomplicated geometric shapes but, although they are quite easily trained, the perfect finish will take a number of years to achieve. The gardener or designer will instinctively know which shape will suit the character of their garden. The sphere, dome or cone are consistently popular and are easy to find in a nursery or garden centre. However, a tier or a cottage loaf is harder to buy ready-grown and would make an easy and pleasing project for a gardener to achieve on their own. The time that it takes to produce a finished piece of topiary can be the reason for choosing to buy, but often the only way to have the exact shape you want is to grow

A topiary shape. Box can be cut to produce sculptural forms with fine detail, and the capacity for the shoots to be trained allows a good deal of flexibility about how the shape is developed.

and train it yourself. If daunted by this, do not despair, because the time can be greatly reduced by sourcing an appropriate unstructured box plant of the right size.

As well as the simple topiary forms that are a mainstay of garden design, there are individual figu-

These are topiary forms of various shapes and sizes. Individual pieces like these cannot always be found in nurseries and the best option may be to produce your own. These topiary specimens were grown at River Garden Nurseries in Kent.

rative shapes that give the topiarist complete freedom to use their own ideas and to introduce their distinctive and individual presence to the garden. These can be exceptional and imposing compositions or they may just be small items for pure amusement. Forming a new piece of topiary from an unshaped plant is rewarding, and when novices are experimenting in workshops it is surprising how quickly their confidence grows. Nevertheless, reassurance is required when the final shape does not appear immediately. It needs time and the plant's natural growth capacity for the shape to emerge and the apprentice topiarist must have the imagination and patience to understand how the box plant will fill out by regeneration. The use of a wire frame in a pre-formed shape might appear to be an easy route to achieve a quick result, but there are various reasons why this technique is unsatisfactory. The wire frame will eventually interfere with the growth and longevity of the plant and it prevents the gardener from shaking out and remov-

ing the natural cycle of dead leaves from the centre of the plant. Wire also makes it more difficult to develop and maintain a good shape as it prevents the topiarist from corrective pruning deep into the growth. Finally, topiary should allow the gardener to enjoy the flight of fancy when creating a figure. Conforming to a pre-ordained shape precludes any spark of originality.

Training box in the ground is always preferable to training in a container. This is because pruning and shaping makes demands on the plant and regrowth will take place more easily in the ground where nutrients are readily available. If possible, the initial shaping should begin in the early spring before the young shoots develop, in order to benefit from the active spring and early summer growth. As a general principle, decisive pruning from the outset will speed the training process and produce the most successfully structured topiary; ambivalence when making the first cuts will be regretted down the line. This is particularly

Nestled into a border is a pair of lovebirds grown out of one plant. This is a very individual piece and is developed from the creative impulse of the topiarist; it would never be found as a stock item.

BELOW: Tools of the trade. Raffia is useful for training topiary figures where soft stems need to be guided in new directions. It has the advantage that it will biodegrade in time.

true for box spirals where the skeleton of the topiary must be established from the outset. The early process of pruning and shaping will make extra demands on the plant to regenerate and, therefore, it is important to marshal the balance of nutrients and water to maintain good growth and a healthy plant. Another general point to be made is the importance of working at a piece of topiary throughout the growing season, not just when first fashioned. As new shoots develop, they should be pinched out to conform to the required shape.

Types of Topiary

A Ball

The box ball is one of the staple items of topiary and it is useful for the gardener to be able to produce this simple shape.

First of all, choose a well-branched plant that will prune neatly to a height that is no more than its width. A ball of any size can be made from the smallest plant, it is just a matter of time as the developing shape is trimmed to keep to the correct proportions. For example, if a small box plant measures 25cm (10in) high and 12cm (4¾in) wide, reduce the height to match the width. The principle is the same whether you begin

ABOVE: A box ball. One of the staple topiary shapes.

with a small or a much larger, unstructured plant. At the early stages of developing the shape, use secateurs to prune rather than shears and reduce any robust growth that will develop faster than the rest – in particular, the thicker, central, leading branches at the apex of the plant. Start the shape in early spring and use the whole growing season to pinch out the tips to consolidate the ball as often as necessary. This is where the technique for training a new shape differs from that for maintaining a mature piece of topiary, where clipping is done just once a year. Making new topiary shapes is not a quick process and it will take a few growing seasons before the gaps fill in and the shape begins to build. Apply an organic fertilizer early in the spring and again in mid-summer, on account of the extreme demands of this regrowth, and be sure to give sufficient water until late autumn.

A Standard or a Mini-Lollipop

Standards are elegant shapes that can be used to frame an entrance, while their clear stems, when repeated in an avenue, make a powerful impact. Mini-standards can be used in small containers with colourful planting.

A box standard. An elegant shape with pleasing visual impact.

Forming a box standard, step 1: initial pruning of a suitable plant with a straight stem.

Forming a box standard, step 2: some growth has been left on the stem to strengthen the plant's further growth.

This shape takes time to mature into a finished piece of topiary because all the development must grow through a single stem. This can be trained in a pot, but there are benefits of growing it in the ground because the process is slow and grounded roots will establish and be more able to support the demands of regeneration. Begin by choosing a suitable box plant with a straight central stem. The advantage in selecting a

Forming a box standard, step 3: the ball is shaped, with work yet to be done at the apex.

early stages, as light growth will strengthen the central leader.

First, stake the central stem and keep the tip growing until the height is reached at which the ball is to be developed. The girth of the stem will develop and thicken annually, but once the growing tip is cut and work begins on shaping the ball, the stem will remain at the same height. The training from this point is to pinch out the tip of the shoots in and around the surface of the ball during the growing season in order to build up the shape. This is not a difficult topiary design but it does require patience to form a perfect ball. When miniature topiary lollipops are designed for small pots on a terrace or for a balcony window-box, they are eye-catching and have the additional advantage that small spring and summer annuals and bulbs can be underplanted at the base of their stem to give a colourful composition.

A Cone

A ubiquitous feature of formal gardens, box cones have many uses for the garden designer.

A cone is one of the simpler shapes to develop, as you are making the most of the natural growth habit of *Buxus sempervirens*. Choose a plant with a well-balanced shape and, ideally, one with a strong central stem and leader. Before beginning the work on the cone ensure that the plant is upright and that its leader is perpendicular, whether in the ground or a pot. Work with both secateurs and shears to form the early cone. By standing above and looking directly down from the apex, use the shears to clip a regular conical shape and use the secateurs to cut the thicker stems. Gradually establish the new shape with the main focus on establishing a balanced growth on either side of the main stem; it is important to achieve a consistent angle. As with all training, secateurs are essential during the early stages because, unlike a pair of shears, which cut along the contour of the surface, secateurs give the gardener more control over the structure of the plant, allowing individual branches to be pruned into shape. During the second season of training there will be enough young growth to gently clip with a pair of hand shears. The height of the cone can be extended each year by training the new growth at the apex, in the spring.

young, strong plant is that the side shoots will be slender and some can be removed without scarring the stem. The aim is to produce a clear stem, but it is important not to remove every young lateral shoot during the

A box cone. A classic shape with many uses.

A box spiral. It will catch the attention wherever it is placed.

A Spiral

A box spiral is an eye-catcher and will be the focus of interest and admiration wherever it is placed in the garden.

Although it may seem rather a waste to use one shape to make another, the best result for making a box spiral will come from using a well-prepared and clipped cone. A shaped cone will make it far easier to produce a well-proportioned spiral. When possible, choose a cone with a straight central stem and multiple fine branches, rather than fewer thick ones. Begin by shaking out the fallen trapped leaves within the plant and disentangling any branches that are caught within the structure. Next, wind raffia in a spiral down the smooth surface of the cone to mark the line for

incision and adjust the curves of the helix until they are evenly spaced apart and parallel to each other. The spacing between the raffia parallel lines will be approximately 20–30cm (8–12in), although the precise width between each spiral will be a matter of proportion, style and the height of the cone. The first step, with secateurs, is to follow the line of the spiralling raffia and to cut into the surface of the cone so that a groove can clearly be seen.

Spiral shapes are quite difficult to establish and it is helpful to work slowly at every stage, standing back in order to take a view of the progress. From the tip of the spiral, work along the line that you have cut to go deeper into the shape. This should be repeated several times until you feel confident that the groove is well established. Remove the raffia at this stage because it will now be less of a help and more of a hindrance when pruning out any branches that interfere with the parallel spacing between each spiral ridge. There will often be the need to cut away thick stems of vertical growth, even though these may be carrying a proportion of branches that were relied upon to make the shape. Without these there will be unavoidable gaps in the spiral but, although the pruning may seem drastic, new growth will build up in time and the reward will be a better constructed figure.

The central stem is an important feature of the spiral and it should be revealed when possible, as this will add to the aesthetic character of the topiary. Carry on working at the corkscrew until you are satisfied that there is good definition from top to bottom. There is a temptation to shape a spiral instantly to look like a fin-ished piece of work, but timid training will result in the spiral losing its shape with the next year's growth. When the work on shaping the spiral has been finished, clip lightly with hand shears, following the line down from top to bottom, to establish the curves and flow. This is a topiary shape that can be extended annually by allow-ing the top shoots to grow and pinching out the tips, gradually working toward forming an additional helix.

A Ball or Dome, Topped with a Bird

A witty piece of topiary that looks well in a container or as a specimen to lighten a corner of the garden.

Forming a box spiral, step 1: a cone shape with raffia drawn around it in a spiral.

Forming a box spiral, step 2: a spiral groove cut into the plant along the line of the raffia, which has been removed.

Choose a bushy, unclipped plant of *Buxus semper-virens* with sufficient upper growth to fashion as a bird. Before beginning to shape, fix a bamboo with a coloured mark to indicate the top of the ball as this will help as a visual guide for the initial shaping. The mark should be approximately two-thirds from the ground to the apex of the plant. Prune back the lower section of the plant that will make the ball to a rounded form using secateurs, ensuring that the thicker growth is cut slightly further back into the outline of the shape so that there will be regular foliage growth at the surface when the growth fills out. There will be many gaps at this stage, but so long as a spherical shape is maintained, these will thicken with young growth in subsequent years. When work on the ball is finished, lightly clip with hand shears all over to encourage new growth.

Now turn your attention to the bird. Begin by identifying the branches that will form the head and the tail, which should be diametrically opposite to each other. It is often the case that the top branches of a box plant will lend themselves toward a particular shape. Tie pieces of raffia to the tip of these branches to avoid accidently snipping off these key structures. Next, shorten the stems around the central body of the bird with secateurs and form the structure of the body into a light, skeletal shape, knowing that the new growth will add flesh to the bones. Position the head to allow for the breast to develop in time. The beak can be formed with malleable young growth and angled into a good position. To do this, tie a thread of raffia around the beak and secure the raffia to a thicker stem below. It can take several attempts before a suitable angle is found. Sometimes the bird topiary can be brought to

Forming a box spiral, step 3: the finished spiral shape, which will fill out in subsequent years.

A ball with bird. It introduces a whimsical touch.

life by pointing the head one way or the other. The tail feathers can be in line with the body or angled upwards in the fashion of a wren; this can also be helped with raffia in order to establish a tilt or a slant. The young growth of box is wonderfully pliable and once a shoot has been trained at an angle, it will hold its line after a few months. Raffia works well because it is biodegradable and will fall away at the end of the first season, after it has been used to tweak and refine the shape. For your final form, the natural world offers no end of examples to inspire the imaginative designer, whether from the local hedgerow or a tropical rainforest!

Forming a ball with bird, step 1: an unshaped bush with a marker indicating the top of the ball.

Forming a ball with bird, step 2: the ball has been pruned and raffia tags indicate the beak and tail of the bird.

A cottage loaf. Brings in an informal touch.

Forming a ball with bird, step 3: keep in mind what foliage will fill in to form the tail, body, breast and head/beak. Do not worry about any gaps at this stage.

A Cottage Loaf

Their rounded forms are very characterful and the cottage loaf lends itself to more informal types of design.

To model a cottage loaf, take an unshaped plant of *Buxus sempervirens* of a suitable size and begin by shaking out the fallen, trapped leaves within the plant and disentangle any branches that are caught within the structure. Snip the growth into a rounded shape using a combination of secateurs and shears. Always have a pair of secateurs at hand when starting any new shape, because the thicker stems within the structure of a box plant will damage your shears.

The base of the cottage loaf will be more substantial than the shape that sits on top and the waist between the two should be indicated by using two marked bamboos. Part of the charm of this design is that it can be informal and asymmetrical and often a little lopsided. Use the shears on the soft growth and secateurs on the thicker stems to form a ledge between the two loaves and gradually round off the surface of the base shape to the waistline. Using shears and secateurs, round the

Forming a cottage loaf, step 1: a bush growing in a border. Markers indicate the level where the junction will be between the two shapes.

top shape into a dimension that is compatible with the base. Topiary of this sort flourishes with a touch of informality and asymmetry, and no two pieces will be the same. Secateurs are the primary tool but at this first stage of development, a light clip with hand shears on all soft growth will smooth the surface. Finally, pinch out the young tips in order to stimulate new growth.

A Pillar with Ball

A pillar with a ball finial is a topiary design that is used exclusively in formal design where it will stand on either side of an entrance, making as strong a statement as a stone pillar.

Having decided on the height and width of the pillar and the diameter of the ball, choose an

Forming a cottage loaf, step 2:
the ledge has been formed between the two parts of the loaf. At this stage, secateurs are the most useful tool for thicker stems. Round the upper and lower parts in proportion.

unshaped box plant that approximately matches the overall proportions of the planned piece of topiary, as this will significantly reduce the time it will take to achieve the shape. Unshaped box plants are available between November and March and are sold as 'root-balled', which means that the root is lifted with soil and contained by a hessian cloth that should be removed before planting in the ground. After plant-ing, plan the pillar by marking the height and the width with bamboo sticks and only prune the growth that falls outside that dimension. Once the pillar has been formed, it is helpful to go over the surface again with secateurs and reduce the thicker stems by a few more centimetres, so that the new shoots grow to form a dense surface to the pillar once they have been clipped.

A pillar with ball. Used for formal entrances.

Fashion the ball to sit on the plane of the pillar so that there is ample rebate at the point where the two shapes join together. Keep the form tight and ensure that the young growth develops in a regular sphere. A

pillar and ball topiary has fine detail and it will take time before there is enough young growth to make the perfect right angles of the pillar. It will also take time for the ball to mature, but once achieved it is a classic and satisfying shape.

Tiered Shape

This formal piece of topiary has its origins in the knot gardens of classical times when it was used as a centrepiece for knot designs. It can be put to the same use today; otherwise, its elegant shape can be used as a point of interest elsewhere in the garden. A good example can be seen in the image that opens this chapter.

The ideal way to construct this shape is to choose a plant that has been loosely formed into a slim cone, as this will give the width at the base for the first tier and enough material above to shape the ascending horizontal plates. A single, straight, central stem is paramount because this will form the dominant vertical trunk, which will be visible from every angle. The height of the cone will decide the number of layers that can be trained in the first year and it is important to allow for each horizontal tier to develop, with enough space between each one to give clear definition.

Working from the base of the cone, use secateurs to shape the first section by pruning any vertical growth hard and allowing horizontal shoots to develop at right angles to the stem. To form the next level, mark the gap between the tiers by tying raffia to the central stem of the cone at the point where the base of the next tier will begin. Again, hard prune the vertical growth, ideally to a bud, and encourage the horizontal growth. Each tier should be an equal distance from the tier below, repeating the tiers until the point is reached where there is insufficient material for shaping. Conclude this stage by identifying a strong leader coming from the central stem that can grow on upwards and eventually set the stage for the next tier.

This is a shape that can be successfully extended year by year, adding tiers until the required height is achieved. The open design allows for easy regeneration and the annual training will keep the tiers compact and encourage horizontal growth, so that the diameter of the discs remains in proportion, with the circumference of each rising tier decreasing in a regular way. An alternative approach is to graduate the distance between the rising tiers so that they become closer as

Topiary pieces of many shapes and sizes on parade after the annual clipping at River Garden Nurseries.

they ascend. However, this limits the number of tiers that can be added in further years.

A Mass Sculptural Form

The property of multiple planting of box to be trimmed into a coherent shape with a sculptural form has been used by contemporary designers in a number of different ways. Monumental green shapes may introduce a feeling of stability to that part of the garden and areas can be linked by using undulating, contours of box. Mass planting can also be positioned at the perimeter of a garden and be allowed to roll gently, mimicking the landscape. Another way in which mass planting can be used in design is by reflecting an architectural feature of a building with the box trimmed to neat, planar surfaces.

These designs are easy to put together and by finding the right-sized plants, the shapes will mature surprisingly quickly. Box plants of all sizes are available through the trade and it is certainly worthwhile to select larger root-balled specimens when setting out a sizeable project. To construct a mass of rounded balls and achieve the effect more quickly, use clipped spherical shapes. Bamboos are helpful in identifying the planting positions and there is a general rule that

Mass-planted box-shape composed of six spheres and gradually grown into one moulded shape.

the distance between the plants should relate to the proposed eventual height, as this will give the plants plenty of space to grow and thrive. For the first year or two allow the plants to establish their roots and put on some growth before allowing your imagination and artistry to develop a shape that fits harmoniously into the surrounding garden.

A Cloud Topiary

This form of topiary is widely practised in Japanese gardens where it is used for symbolic effect, whereby a miniature shape represents an ideal form of a larger object. The classic example is, of course, the bonsai, when a perfectly trimmed small bush mimics a giant tree, but box can also be trimmed to represent other natural features, such as a cloudscape. The strong character of this design needs the right setting in a garden and if well positioned it will be the focus of attention. The small box leaf allows the forms to be trimmed into perfect cloud shapes and the structure of a box plant is suited to the early training of the spreading branches.

In the same way as for beginning any new topiary design, it is helpful to start with a box plant of a suitable height and width. When choosing the plant, look at its structure and check that there are some younger branches that are flexible enough to be trained at an angle. The older and thicker branches are more rigid and will not respond to being trained into the angle required for a well-balanced specimen. Unlike some other shapes that can be developed either in a pot or the ground, this shape should be grown in a nursery bed because the leverage of the branches can only be done by fixing pegs into the ground and attaching twine to realign branches in the required way. What seems casual in a finished specimen has often been achieved with a great deal of effort.

Begin by selecting the pliable stems for the main structure that have suitable side branches for developing a cloud. Identify each of these chosen main stems with a tie of raffia to remind yourself that they should be preserved, before pruning out all the remaining branches, including the ones that are most stiff, thick and upright. There are no rules as to how many main stems are chosen but it is important to focus on how the clouds will form. Each stem will have branching at the apex and these are trimmed into a shape that can grow on to imitate a small cloud. Sometimes there is space to develop a secondary cloud on the same stem by allowing a smaller branch to grow out at an angle and carry a cloud at its apex. Each cloud should have ample room to develop and broaden out into an attractive shape that encapsulates the calm presence of a cumulus cloud. The flexible main branches are trained at the chosen angle by anchoring them with a soft tie that is secured to the ground with a peg. Treat the selected stems in the same way as with a box standard topiary and leave a feathering of young growth along the stem for a year or two, in order to strengthen the developing structure.

A cloud shape developed from one box plant.

CHAPTER 7

CARE, MAINTENANCE AND CLIPPING

For box plants to flourish and remain healthy, the same standards of husbandry apply as they do to all successful gardening – a watchful eye and an awareness of the strength and vigour of the plant. In adverse circumstances box does not show decline immediately and it can take some months before there are obvious signs of distress. Therefore, the focus should be on monitoring the conditions to prevent problems and, should they develop, to put them right as quickly as possible after discovering the cause. Maintaining the best possible situation for growth is particularly important because a healthy box plant is more resistant to disease, particularly from fungal infections.

There are a number of reasons why a box plant might not thrive and in most cases there is a remedy if action is taken in sufficiently good time. The signs are seen in the colour and appearance of the leaves; however, it is often the roots that hold the key to the treatment and cure. Sometimes, the cause is understood if you are aware of the history of the particular plant. For instance, after box has been lifted and replanted, the root disturbance can cause a period of distress that results in a yellowing of the leaves. This is commonly observed in recently planted, bare-rooted hedging that has been lifted without soil and is likely to suffer from desiccation and lack of nutrients until it has established itself. With careful watering until late autumn, the bare-rooted plant will settle into the new planting position. Plants lifted in a root ball are usually spared this problem. On the whole, the gardener can be assured that healthy box is an enormously resilient, long-lived plant that requires little in the way of maintenance. However, in recent years infections and infestations have become a considerable problem to growers of box and the long-term health of plants depends on the detection and treatment of these troubles at the earliest possible stage. However, keeping plants in a healthy condition does a great deal to resist diseases, particularly those caused by fungal infections. The topic of pests and diseases is dealt with in Chapter 8.

General Care

Care of the soil and annual maintenance are important if box plants are to remain in good condition. Clipped topiary and hedging, because of the demands put on it for re-growth, have an added need for nurture.

pH

Box grows best in a calcareous soil with a pH of 6.8 to 7.5. For soils that are more acidic than this, it is recommended that lime is added before planting so that the plants can derive the necessary nutrients from the soil. Dolomitic lime is recommended and when improving acidic soils, mushroom compost is useful because it contains chalk, which has the added advantage of raising the pH. However, alkaline materials should not be used if the soil pH is neutral or high. Soil pH measurement is advised if there is any doubt about the pH status.

Health of the Roots

The roots of box grow wide and shallow, and the plant does better without competition from the roots of adjacent trees and shrubs. The planting of small shrubs and perennial plants will not cause problems, but trees and shrubs with invasive roots will interfere with box and take up valuable nutrients. When box is planted close to any solid underground structure, such as the foundations of a building or a wall, the roots will be restricted from spreading out and developing. In this situation, it would be advisable to keep the height of box plants to a relatively low level, as well as watering diligently and applying additional organic fertilizer.

The health of roots depends on circulation of air and this is impeded by compacted soil and when the ground is waterlogged. Box will not thrive if the soil is too wet and, if this is the case, steps should be taken to install a drainage system. For soil that is too dry, such as sandy soil that drains rapidly, it is best to mix in organic matter to help retain water. A watering system can also be considered, although this needs to be regulated carefully to prevent over-watering.

Fertilizing

Having the correct nutrients is essential for the healthy growth of the plant and it is important to look after the soil by cultivating with organic matter. Feeding with garden compost, well-rotted manure and leaf mould are good for soil structure and fertility and they make the nutrients in the soil available to the plant. Chalky and sandy soils are lower in nutrients and they have a particular need for enrichment by the addition of these soil conditioners. Gardeners often assume that poor growth is related to lack of specific soil nutrients and apply synthetic fertilizer to the ground. However, shortages of plant nutrients in the soil are

quite rare and poor growth is usually due to various environmental factors, including drought, waterlogging and disease. Synthetic fertilizers are a concentrated and short-term source of nutrients, which feed the plant rather than feeding the soil in a sustainable fashion. It is better to improve the soil with organic material and enable the available nutrients already present to be released when the organic material decomposes as a result of the action of microorganisms. A slow-release organic fertilizer, such as bonemeal, can certainly be added to the soil when planting to help establish the roots and a light top dressing, such as fish, blood and bone, can be applied as part of the annual cycle of care.

Nitrogen is very soluble and will be easily washed away from the soil during the winter and deficiency is not uncommon when box is putting on new growth in the spring, particularly after a very wet winter. The symptom of nitrogen deficiency is a lack-lustred appearance of the leaves, which lose their depth of colour. An application of fish, blood and bone and well-rotted garden compost or manure should solve the deficiency. It is worth remembering that box is a slow-growing plant and only moderate amounts of nitrogen are required for healthy growth; high-nitrogen fertilizers should not be added as an accelerant. Other mineral deficiencies are unusual in ground-grown box, although they are not uncommonly seen in box plants grown in containers. These problems are discussed in Chapter 5.

Mulching

There is a strong argument for applying a layer of mulch to the ground around box plants because of its beneficial effect on nutrition and health. Mulching is an effective way of conserving moisture in the soil during the summer and it also suppresses the growth of weeds. In addition, it has been shown that a layer of mulch dramatically reduces fungal infection by inhibiting splash-back of soil inoculum and thereby preventing infection of the plant by entry of spores through the stomata of the lower leaves. There are a variety of organic mulches that are suitable to use with box and these include garden compost, fine wood chip and decomposed leaf mould. The use of woody mulches was controversial but it is now thought that, although they may deprive the surface layer of the soil of nutrients, particularly nitrogen, there is no evidence that this is a problem for established root systems. Mulching the ground is a job to do in the late winter or early spring when conditions are at their best for retaining the soil moisture and avoiding frost.

An alternative to mulching for suppressing weeds is to lay landscaping fabric in and around a box design and cover with decorative gravel or other material. However, this should only be a temporary solution because, although the ground covering solves the problem of weed control, it prevents the application of granular feed and the ability to improve the soil.

Watering

Box is generally tolerant of warm and dry conditions because the thick, waxy epidermis of the leaves excels in water retention. However, plants that have recently been transplanted need to be watered until their roots are well established. One sign of a dehydrated plant is a glaucous discolouration to the young leaves. Box plants that are grown in a very free-draining soil, such as sand, have an increased demand for water and it may be necessary to consider a watering system. If it is decided to install an automatic irrigation system because of the nature of the soil or an arid climate, it is best to choose a trickle system that moistens the soil. Sprinkler irrigation that wets the leaves is likely to lead to foliar disease and is not recommended. Whichever system is used, it is important to monitor the moisture of the ground and manage the amount of watering because box roots can be damaged by over-saturated soil. In temperate climates and good soil conditions, watering is not necessary once the plant is established.

Plant Hygiene

There are some tasks that are worth putting on your list to do once a year when clipping and handling your box. Any form of trimmed box, but particularly topiary, will develop a dense inner structure, which becomes a receptacle for debris, the product of fallen leaves and clipped twigs. This detritus increases the risk of infection by fungal diseases and it is important to put your hands inside the clipped box and clear out anything that has accumulated. This will not only reduce the chance of disease but also increase the air and light circulation, which will improve the general health of the plant.

The young leaves of a dehydrated box plant have a glaucous, blue-green discolouration. This *Buxus sempervirens* was watered and it returned to good health before damage was done.

Nurture

Box is susceptible to a number of diseases and the way in which the plant is grown and nurtured can influence the way it resists these problems. Plants that have better exposure to light and improved circulation of air will grow well and are better able to combat disease, particularly infections from fungi. One way to do this is to maintain a box hedge at a narrow width, so that there is increased air flow through the structure. It is important not to crowd plants when setting out a box design and to keep a good distance between them (*see* Chapter 5).

A box hedge trimmed to be thinner than a standard hedge. The intention is that the increased air-circulation and exposure to light will make a healthier plant that is resistant to disease.

Traditionally, yew and box hedges in formal gardens were clipped with a batter and this was to allow light to reach the bottom of the hedge. This is particularly important if the hedge has a wide base when a slight batter is helpful in sustaining the bushiness of the growth. A hedge with a batter is shown at Restoration House (pp.121–123).

Clipping

For gardeners with box topiary and hedging, the annual clipping is a rite that is anticipated with pleasure. There is an element of a ritual about it, with the careful sharpening of the dedicated fine shears, which have been protected from rougher work around the garden and are now ready to transform the shaggy outlines of the waiting shapes into sculpted precision.

When to Clip

It is often said that box should be clipped by Derby Day, at the beginning of June, but, like everything in the garden, the timing will depend on how the season is developing and the particular conditions in the place where you live. Box begins to put on new growth early in the spring. The new growth has normally developed and hardened off by late May, with the leaves turning to a deeper colour and this indicates that the main growing period of the year is complete. The timing of your clipping may be affected by a late spring frost, which damages the young growth if it occurs when the leaves are soft and tender. These pale and delicate leaves are only at this stage for a very short period, but during this time they are extremely vulnerable and if frosted they will die back and eventually become dry and wrinkled and fall away. Although frustrating, this is only a small setback because new growth will replace the damaged leaves and the only consequence is that the clipping will have to be delayed until this secondary growth catches up with the first flush in order to avoid a patchwork appearance, as would be the case if you clipped twice.

It may be tempting to clip frequently during the growing season to maintain a smooth surface; however, constant clipping will weaken a plant, leading to a gradual decline. Repeated removal of young emerging foliage will prompt the plant to regenerate to sustain growth and expend energy unnecessarily. Box topiary and hedging need only be clipped once in the year, although a second clip can take place in August to tidy the light secondary growth. This should be a quick tidy-up to the few sprigs on the surface so that the box

will have a smooth and neat finish, which will look particularly good when frost or snow decorates the
surface. A harder clipping is not advisable because it
can encourage late growth, which is susceptible to an
early frost.

Clipping Box

Clipping a Parterre or Hedge
Although the work required with clipping large box
designs may be considerable, the anticipation of the
reward of neatly clipped parterres and topiary makes it

worthwhile. A certain amount of planning is required,
but with an established box garden it is a matter of slip-
ping into a well-worked routine. A fine example of a
carefully maintained parterre is seen at Restoration
House, Rochester in Kent and the sequence showing
its preparation and clipping makes a good demonstra-
tion of the best technique for this demanding job. (The
author is grateful to the forbearance of the house's
owners as well as the gardeners, for allowing the photography of the work in 2021.)

There is no doubt that clipping box by hand is superior to using power-assisted shears. Clipping with

Before beginning to clip a box
hedge, it is important to prepare
by laying out ground cover to
catch the clippings and to set up
guide lines to ensure an
accurate cut.

shears avoids damage to the leaves and produces a better finish because the technique makes the hedge more compact. Also, hand-clippers can judge their actions more carefully because they are watching one cut at a time. Unfortunately, many gardeners are not able to indulge in the satisfaction of hand-clipping because it takes longer than the mechanical method. However, using a fuel- or electric-powered machine does come at a price because mechanical shears damage some of the leaves, which are torn by the blades and turn brown. The effects of mechanical clipping are not sufficient to spoil the appearance of a box hedge, but there is no doubt that the result is inferior to that of hand-clipping.

Before starting, begin by eyeing what needs to be clipped and take note of any part that requires corrective pruning to improve the shape. Also, gently ruffle the leaves to release and pull to the surface any small branches that have become straggly and are trapped inside the plant. Once pulled to the surface these strands can be clipped with the rest of the plant and the inner structure will be strengthened and less likely to open up and gape as the box grows in size. Sheets of ground cover should be laid at the base of the topiary or along the hedge and most of the clippings will be collected in this way. What is left under the plant can be raked out and removed.

For short lengths of hedging, it is possible to rely on the eye for confirming that the line is correct by standing back regularly to scrutinize the work and running the eye along the line of the hedge. With a longer run of hedging, it is important to maintain an absolutely uniform height and it is essential to use a stretched cord as a guide line to ensure an even cut. This needs to be set up carefully – nylon is particularly suitable because of its elasticity, which allows it to be kept tense during clipping, so long as it is well secured at both ends. By using shears it is possible to cut precisely to the line and leave a very straight edge. Done with this degree of precision and care, the result is impressive but it does take time – the two gardeners at Restoration House took a total of 100 hours to achieve the final result. The Restoration House parterre is cut with a slight batter, which gives a neat appearance with tapered sides and a narrowed top to the hedges. A batter will also improve the health of the box by increasing the light penetrating the foliage.

Clipping along a guide line ensures a perfectly straight cut.

Clipping Established Box Topiary

In preparation, lay a ground sheet around the base of the specimen in order to collect the clippings. Also ensure that your tools are sharp and when using hand shears have water and a cloth alongside in order to clean off the build-up of sap on the blades. The importance of razor-sharp blades cannot be over-emphasized and the sharpness of hand shears should be regularly checked. The annual clip is an excellent time to carry out the invaluable maintenance job of shaking out dead leaves that may be trapped within the structure of the plant.

When clipping a piece of topiary, the aim is to trim evenly and maintain the shape by following the established angles or curves. One of the advantages of box is that it will hold its form and, because there is little annual growth, the job of clipping is a quite straightforward task. Topiary can be available in many shapes and a novice gardener should be reassured that it is hardly more difficult to follow the lines of a complicated creation than to maintain the shape of a ball, although a little more concentration is required. Whatever shape of topiary is being clipped, look carefully at the whole picture as you progress and work from side-to-side in order to gradually achieve a perfect finish.

The leaves should be cleared away from the surface of the topiary on to the sheeting as the clipping progresses. As you clip, stand back regularly to view the item afresh from all angles. Once the job is done, brush off any clipped leaves and this process may release a stem of two that have been trapped; these can then be trimmed as well. After you have finished, it is important to remove all the fallen clippings. To avoid the risk of fungal infection, debris should not be composted but burned or disposed of through the local authority garden waste system. Another important precaution when clipping a number of topiary shapes is to regularly disinfect the shears to avoid spreading disease.

ABOVE: Clipping the parterre at Restoration House. The job is nearly complete and with meticulous attention to detail, a long run of guide lines have been set up to ensure that the last small section of the design is cut accurately.

The final result. Note the batter cut into the sides of the parterre, which is outlined by the shadowing.

Different forms of topiary require different techniques from the topiarist. With cones and spirals, it is possible to maintain their shape but at the same time allow them to grow a little taller each year. Instead of clipping off the leading shoots, it is possible to allow the shape to continue to grow upwards. To do this, tie the pinched-out shoots together with a strand of raffia, so that they establish themselves as a new apex. This will have happened by the time the raffia has biodegraded and has served its purpose. With smaller cones, it helps to clip from above, looking downwards so that your eye can use the leader as your guide to the symmetry of the cone. When clipping a rounded shape, it is useful to use the angled shape of hand shears to your advantage by reversing the shears. Some topiarists find the use of frames helpful, particularly those with collections of identical geometrical shapes, such as four-sided pyramids that need to be clipped to the same size. Place the frame over the topiary and clip to the shape that will give a consistent angle on each side. A purpose-made, light, wooden frame, which is constructed to the required form, can be removed once the clipping is complete and kept in store until it is time for next year's outing.

Clipping a Knot

All knot gardens have interlinking, low hedges that make up the design. The way that the hedges are cut varies according to the impression that it is intended to achieve. Knots that are similar to the *La Maison Rustique* design have a flowing, over–under effect and the topiarist should achieve a dynamic appearance by moulding the shape to give a feeling of continuous motion with rounded curves. Other knots do not have over–unders at the junctions and the hedges are cut flat. The low hedges should be kept to a width of approximately 25–30cm (10–12in).

Tools Used for Clipping

The choice of tools used for clipping box depends on a number of factors, including the amount of time available for the job, the quality of the result and the complexity of the piece to be clipped. Hand shears will be favoured for a complex task and when the best result is desired, but the time-saving properties of mechanical shears establish their place as an essential tool.

Hand Shears

The aim in clipping box is to achieve a neatly cut, smooth surface. The tool that is used to bring this about is worth attention because it will make a difference to the success of the result and the enjoyment of achieving it. A good pair of shears is a precision instrument and a joy to use. In many gardens there will be a mixture of hedges to clip, including box, yew and other shrubs, and there should be a choice of shears in the tool shed because it is important to keep a pair of hedge-cutters for dealing with the heavier and coarser work, while other shears should be dedicated to fine work such as box. If the garden includes box hedges as well as topiary pieces, it is best to have at least two shears with different lengths of blade for work on box because rounded shapes, such as balls and spirals, are easier to clip with a short blade, while a large box design or a parterre with a lengthy run will be easier with a longer blade. There is also the choice between different types of blade. A wavy blade will give good control when clipping thick growth by firmly griping the leaves and stems, and limiting movement as the

It is often helpful to have more than one length of shears to deal with different shapes of topiary.

edges come together, while the straight blade is most satisfactory for fine clipping. The weight and balance of the tool will vary enormously and the decision about which pair to choose is a matter for the individual. It is helpful to handle the shears before purchasing in order to be sure that the balance of the tool is right for you. The shears should feel comfortable and the cutting motion easy and unforced, so that there is no strain, with the tool giving the feeling that it is an effortless extension of the arm. The weight of the shears is important and the lighter they are, the better for long periods of clipping. Having a rubber end-stopper to cushion the stroke is also a help. Modern tools that are favoured by professional topiarists on account of their weight, the superior quality of the blades and precision of engineering, include those manufactured by ARS, Bahco, Bardel and Niwaki. It is extremely important to maintain your shears during and at the end of clipping.

Powered Shears

The advantage of electric over petrol hedge-clippers is that they are lighter in weight with no fumes and less noise. Electrical shears that are powered by a rechargeable battery are favoured for all but the heaviest work and the disadvantage of a limited supply of energy can be overcome by having two batteries, alternating the one in use with one on charge. An electric clipper with a mains cable is limited by the length of its cable and the operator must keep it away from the blades by leading it through a loop in the belt at the back of the body, so there is some restriction in movement. The cable should always be connected to the mains via an RCD circuit breaker and should never be used in wet weather. In favour of petrol clippers is their power and the advantage that they can be used for cutting hedges with a mixture of thick growth, rather than the normal light annual growth of box.

Maintaining Your Shears

- Clean the blades. Remove the sap that builds up along the edge of the blade by cleaning with water, rubbing clean with a nail brush and wiping with a towel. This should be done regularly during and after clipping.
- Lightly lubricate the blades.
- Sharpen your shears regularly by whetting each in turn with a small diamond file by following the angle of the bevel. Remove the burr on the flat, inside of the blade with one smooth sweep. Apply a little oil to the central joint. An annual sharpening when the blades are disassembled, mounted in a vice and sharpened with a grinder to reset the edge, may be required if use has been exceptional. A way of testing whether shears are sharp and well aligned is to cut through a sheet of paper. A clean cut is an indication that they are in good condition.

RIGHT: Sharpening a pair of shears with a diamond file.

Maintaining the Structure of Clipped Box

Retrieving a Mature Box Shape

After some years of regular clipping, a large box shape can begin to collapse and develop deep clefts in the foliage. This happens when the weak internal branches are no longer able to support the weight of the exterior green growth. If you part the branches you will see brittle stems with virtually no leaf activity in the interior of the plant. This is caused by inadequate light. The remedy is to find where the weight of compressed branches is dragging the topiary apart and to prune out stems of approximately 15–20cm (6–8in) in order to reduce some of the strain. Sunlight will aid the regeneration of the plant and fill in with new growth. This can be done in early winter and with a subsequent feed in the spring the plant will be ready to put on new growth.

Thinning a Box Hedge or Shape

Some types of box with a dense growth habit will at times benefit from being thinned. *Buxus sempervirens* 'Suffruticosa' was often chosen for low hedging and knot gardens because of its attractive small leaves and compact growth. 'Suffruticosa' is an example of a box that, after years of clipping, can have growth on the exterior but poor internal leaf growth and a weakened branching system. Poor air circulation and reduced light can lead to increased moisture and the development of *Volutella* and *Macrophoma*. To encourage internal growth, prune into the plant and remove small branches from the thickest areas of growth. This is an early winter job that will improve the hedge and make it ready for new growth in the spring.

An unsightly cleft has developed in this large box ball because the internal branches are no longer able to support the weight of the exterior growth.

Reclaimed shape after pruning out branches to reduce the weight. In this case, the action had immediate effect.

Thin a dense plant with poor internal growth by pruning branches of about 15cm (6in) length.

CHAPTER 8

BOX PESTS AND DISEASES

The Problem of Pest and Disease in a Box Garden

Box is a much-loved presence in so many gardens and it has a role that no other plant can fill in such a satisfactory way. Sadly, in the last twenty-five years there has been a price to pay for continuing to enjoy this pleasure because it is vulnerable to two significant problems that have appeared during this time. These can have a devastating effect on plants and, if no action is taken, whole gardens can be affected. The first to appear was box blight, a fungus that was noticed in a single nursery in the south of England in 1994 and since then has been seen throughout Asia, Europe, North America, Australia and New Zealand. Just at the time when gardeners and growers of box were becoming reconciled to the depredations of blight, a new pest, the box tree caterpillar, arrived in Europe from East Asia, facilitated by the global nature of trade and extensive transport networks. The box tree caterpillar was probably imported by sea to German inland ports in wood packaging of natural stone products in 2006. Since then it has spread extensively throughout Europe from the region of the German/Swiss border and has had a very harmful effect on box plants, both growing wild and in gardens, although it is not a concern in its native land where a natural predator, a parasitic wasp,

Chelonus tabonus, keeps it under control. Unfortunately, there is no natural predator in other countries and the birds that feed on similar prey appear to find it unpalatable. Although jackdaws, as well as blue tits, have been seen feeding on it, this has not had any significant effect on the spread of the caterpillar. The European Boxwood and Topiary Society (EBTS) does excellent work in tracking outbreaks of the infestation in the United Kingdom and Europe, and a 'hot spot' map can be seen on their website (www.ebts.org/bmctracker/). In November 2018, the moth crossed the Atlantic and was reported in Toronto. In May 2021, plants thought to be contaminated with box tree moth were distributed from a nursery in Canada to retail facilities in seven states in the USA.

The gardener has to take a view about these threats and two approaches are open. The first is to despair of box altogether and to uproot affected as well as healthy plants. The disappointment of seeing damage to a much-loved display, and dismay at the difficulties with continuing in the presence of a threat for which there is, at present, no permanent solution, are certainly daunting. The second approach is to be reconciled with these threats, which, although considerable, can be managed. The price that has to be paid for continuing to have box in the garden is to take prophylactic action against the disease in order to reduce the chances of being affected, to be vigilant in spotting disease and to be meticulous in treating any outbreak that occurs. Having box in the garden does require effort and the willingness to jump into action as soon as a problem is detected, but the benefits are considerable. Many gardeners who have grown to love box would find it unimaginable to banish it from their garden.

General Measures to Control Disease

The best way to reduce the chances of being affected by box diseases and infestations is to keep plants vigorous and healthy. Attention should be given to providing plants with the correct hydration and nutrition (see Chapter 7) and every gardener should have an annual maintenance cycle to attend to their needs. Keeping plants healthy has two advantageous effects. First, it increases the resistance to disease and, second, if plants have been attacked, the natural resilience of box will lead to regrowth and this will be more vigorous if the stems are in good health. As well as good nutrition, with attention to soil pH, mineral content, organic matter and hydration, care should be taken to provide a suitable environment for growth. Because most box diseases are fungal, they develop and spread more readily in dank conditions, which should be avoided. Hedging plants should have adequate space between each other and should not be overhung by plantings of perennials and annuals. It is recommended that box is not clipped in wet weather because this also encourages movement of spores to other areas. Reduce moisture within the plant by thinning the growth so that there is good circulation of air. The beneficial effects of a layer of mulch to prevent splash-back of soil inoculum are discussed in Chapter 7.

Hygiene measures should be applied meticulously to your practice of cultivation. Spores can be transmitted by garden tools and these should be cleaned and disinfected with a mild disinfectant solution before and after use on box. Disease can remain dormant for long periods of time and it is important to suspect its presence, even when not visible. Great care should be taken to remove debris, which might contain disease, after you have cleaned out diseased parts of the plant. Lay out sheeting around the plant, shake and rake it out and clear away debris from under the canopy. The debris should be collected and burned or binned and not put

into compost because of the risk of re-infection; infected elements have considerable powers of endurance, with spores lying dormant for several years.

In order to reduce the chances of introducing disease into your garden, strict standards of hygiene should be applied and every new plant imported from outside should be regarded as a potential source of contagion. There is an argument for enforcing a period of quarantine on imported plants, but the full implications of this have to be thought through. Whereas four weeks might be sufficient when conditions of high temperature and humidity are optimal for the development of disease, at other times problems may take much longer to manifest. Professional and scientific facilities generally apply a period of one year. Of course, the ideal approach is to produce new plants from your own healthy cuttings, although this is not always practical. Bare-rooted hedging plants should always be separated and healed in to soil, rather than being stored in a moist condition.

Susceptibility of Different Species and Cultivars of Box to Pests and Diseases

In the search for an answer to the problem of box pests and diseases, it has been considered whether certain *Buxus* species or cultivars might be more resistant than others. The Royal Horticultural Society (RHS) has carried out a research project at their field research station at Deers Farm to discover whether *B. sempervirens*, *B. sempervirens* 'Suffruticosa' or *B. microphylla* var. *japonica* 'Faulkner' are affected differently with regard to egg-laying by the box moth, *Cydalima perspectalis*. It was found that the 'Faulkner' cultivar was significantly less affected than the others and this is in line with anecdotal reports that it is relatively resistant to this infestation. The same study carried out by the RHS found that the architectural shape that a box plant was cut to (sphere or cube) and the severity with which it was pruned (minimal to heavy pruning and thinning) had no effect on the propagation of eggs.

Research has also been carried out into the resistance of certain cultivars and hybrids to box blight and it was found that a number of them, including 'Faulkner', 'John Baldwin', 'Belvédère', 'Tide Hill', 'National' and 'Trompenburg' were less prone to infection than others. For these reasons, demand for 'Faulkner' has

Box Pests and Diseases

Name of disease or pest	Type	Name of pathogen	Main features of identification
Box blight	Fungus	Calonectria henricotiae/ C. pseudonaviculata	Brown, fallen leaves with white fungus underneath. Bare stems with black streaks on young wood.
Volutella blight	Fungus	Pseudonectria buxi	Yellowed leaves with pink spots underneath in early stages. Leaves fall later.
Box rust	Fungus	Puccinia buxi	Thickened rusty blisters on both sides of leaves. Not a serious pathogen.
Macrophoma leaf spot	Fungus	Macrophoma candollei	Tiny, black spots on yellow, dying leaves. A weak pathogen. Found inside box hedges.
Root rot	Oomycete (fungus-like)	Phytophthora	Yellow, sparse, diminutive foliage throughout shrub. Severely pruned root system. Occurs in poorly drained soil.
Box tree caterpillar	Insect	Cydalima perspectalis	Green-yellow caterpillars. White loose webbing; cocoon that conceals pupae. Pale-yellow, flattish eggs on leaves.
Psyllid	Insect	Psylla buxi	Cup-shaped leaves. In spring, white waxy material on leaves. The green adult can measure up to 3mm (⅒in).
Box leaf-mining gall midge	Insect	Monarthropalpus flavus	Yellowish oval discolouration on upper leaf surface, swelling on lower leaf surface. Leaf abscission if there is more than three midge per leaf. Rare in UK.
Mussel scale	Insect	Lepidosaphes ulmi	Blackish-brown shells or scales shaped like mussels up to 3mm (⅒in) in length on the stems of plants.
Box red spider mite	Insect	Eurytetranychus buxi	Fine, whitish mottling on leaves. No serious damage to plants. More common in sunny sites.

undoubtedly increased among gardeners. Unfortunately, it has large leaves and a loose rather than compact habit, which makes it less suitable for hedging and topiary, where a fine-grained finish is required.

The table shows a list of the main fungi and insects that affect *Buxaceae*, together with their appearance. Further details about the more important box pests and diseases are given in the text.

Box Blight and Other Fungal Infections

Box Blight

Box blight is caused by two closely related fungi, *Calonectria henricotiae* and *Calonectria pseudona-viculata*. The previous name for box blight was *Cylindrocladium buxicola*, which is a synonym for *Calonectria pseudonaviculata* and has been superseded by the present terminology.

Box blight affects box leaves and stems, and the most common method of introducing blight to a garden is by bringing in infected plants from outside. Once there, it is usually spread by direct contagion between plants or by an agent, particularly the human agent, which carries the fungus from one plant to another. The spores of box blight are sticky and are able to adhere to potential carriers, so transmission around the garden may occur by transfer on infected material, such as the soil on boots, and on garden implements. Research has shown that water splash is responsible for carrying infected material from the ground up into the leaves where it enters through the

A hedge affected by box blight. The leaves are blackened and leaf fall has occurred.

stomata. Simply pruning the foliage up to 10–15cm (4–6 in) from the ground virtually eliminates what is the most common cause of infection.

Another measure that has been shown to reduce attacks of blight is the laying of mulch around the roots of planted box. A research study carried out by Virginia Tech in their field unit in Hamptons Road, Virginia, USA, showed that plants of B. sempervirens 'Justin Brouwers' grown in mulched conditions had as much as 97 per cent fewer attacks of blight. The reasoning is that the presence of mulch provides a barrier that prevents splashed water from the ground from creating damp conditions and carrying an inoculum upward into the canopy of the plant and causing disease. Suitable mulches include fine bark and garden compost; commercial products are also available.

Transmission of spores by bird and insect vectors also occurs and outbreaks of infection may be transferred from one garden to another, with no other connection between the two. It is also possible that these vectors may play a part in spreading infections around the local area. Box blight is resistant to frost and, since spores can survive in the ground for at least six years, it may seem to appear from nowhere, even after it has been thoroughly eradicated. Box blight is most prevalent when there are warm and damp conditions, which are favourable for its propagation. The importance of maintaining a healthy plant in a suitable environment as a means of preventing outbreaks of box blight should be emphasized.

Identifying Box Blight

Box plants affected by box blight have small brown to black specks that enlarge to discrete spots or diffuse blotches up to 1cm (½in) in diameter. The centres of the spots become tan with an outer ring of black, necrotic tissue. A yellow, orange or red halo sometimes develops around the spots. Infected leaves fall, resulting in an accumulation of leaf litter under the plant. Young stems are affected by brown or black streaks that are 1–3mm (up to 1/10in) wide, by 1–30mm (up to 1 3/16in) long. As box blight progresses, defoliation occurs, the stems appear bare and the canopy sparse.

Treatment of Box Blight

The importance of having healthy and vigorous plants cannot be over-emphasized and all steps should be taken to improve the nutrition of plants and to provide them with a healthy environment. As soon as box blight has been identified, diseased parts of the plant should be cut back to healthy stems with green wood under the bark. This should be done without delay and it is important to be as radical as needed, not worrying about how much of the plant is removed, because roots are not affected by box blight and re-growth will even generate from the main stem, although the time

Brown-centred lesions with a black surround indicate infection with box blight, *Calonectria henricotiae/ C. pseudonaviculata*.

Damage from box blight with black streaks on stems and brown leaves.

taken to regain the previous height will obviously depend on how much is taken off. Local action can be taken against a small area of disease, but if a hedge or parterre is affected more extensively, a better final result is often achieved by reducing the height in a uniform fashion, cutting away to half the height or more. Healthy box has extraordinary regenerative capacity and in the growing season, new shoots will be apparent within a short time after pruning.

Great care must be taken to clear the dead material because it may contain viable spores and will be a source of re-infection. After clearing diseased plant material, the area can be sprayed with a fungicide, making sure to cover thoroughly and to include as much of the underside of leaves and those as close to the ground as possible. Suitable preparations for box blight are available, with product label recommendations; these can be used several times a year, according to manufacturer's recommendations. Instructions include avoiding spraying when rain is expected and also in bright sunshine and when plants are very dry.

Other Fungi Affecting Box

Volutella Blight
Another fungus that commonly affects box is Volutella blight caused by *Pseudonectria buxi*. This is a less serious problem than box blight and will not devastate

A box hedge affected by Volutella blight.

The stems have been pruned to the level of healthy stems. The step at the right side of the picture shows how much has been removed. Pruning continued until an even level was achieved.

plants or cause widespread leaf fall. Identification of Volutella blight is by noting diseased leaves with yellow appearance and some leaf-fall, but the stems do not develop the black, streaky appearance of *Calonectria henricotiae/Calonectria pseudonaviculata*. Examination of the underside of leaves reveals spores that may be pink in high-humidity environments, while the spores of box blight are white. Management of Volutella blight is first and foremost to maintain a healthy plant in a supportive growing environment, because box plants are only prey to Volutella blight in unfavourable conditions. Chemical control is not necessary, and if disease

There was re-growth of healthy box six weeks after the plant had been pruned.

BELOW RIGHT: A mature box tree moth caterpillar, *Cydalima perspectalis*, which can grow to 4cm (1½in) in length. Its lifespan is approximately four weeks (depending on temperature) before becoming a pupa, then a moth.

does occur, it should be treated by cutting out and thinning to improve the air circulation. Thinning is an important part of disease prevention and mitigation; this is discussed further in Chapter 7.

Macrophoma Leaf Spot

Box is also affected by Macrophoma leaf spot, which is not a virulent disease and a healthy plant will usually resist infection. Macrophoma only affects weakened plants and is classified as a secondary parasite. Infection causes tiny, raised black spots on leaves, which are best treated by pruning the infected branches. Good air-circulation will help the health of the plant and thinning dense foliage is recommended. Sanitation, by removing infected foliage from around the plant, is also important.

Pests Affecting *Buxus*

Box Tree Caterpillar

The box tree caterpillar (*Cydalima perspectalis*) has the capacity to devastate box plants very suddenly. There are reports that this can occur overnight, but it is likely that earlier signs of infestation have been neglected and plants have not been inspected on a regular basis.

However, once an infestation with the caterpillar has taken hold, the voracious insects can do extensive damage very quickly. The more vigilant the gardener is prepared to be, the better the outcome that can be expected. When caterpillar attacks are managed at an early stage, the plants will recover quickly, with new leaf growth from the healthy stems. The impact of box moth caterpillars has been devastating in the areas affected, not only in domestic culture of box but also in natural box woodlands, particularly in Germany, Bulgaria, Romania, north-west Italy, the Basque country of Spain and southern France. It is now established in large regions of the UK, particularly London and south-east England. Spread is believed to be largely from the commercial movement of products containing eggs or developmental forms of the pest, rather than flight of the moth itself. However, the box moth is known to fly as far as 10km (6 miles) and may be responsible for spread within a local area.

Life Cycle of Box Tree Moth

Understanding the biology of *Cydalima perspectalis* helps in the control of the insect because preventative measures can be applied when they are most effective. The life cycle of the box tree caterpillar lasts approximately forty-five days from egg to mature moth and the duration at critical stages depends on sufficient temperature. The temperature threshold for the development of pupae is greater than 11.5°C. Eggs are greenish-yellow and flattish, 1mm (1/32in) diameter and are laid on the leaf where they have the appearance of plaques of stacked coins. Developing eggs have a black dot where the larval head is growing and it takes three days to emerge as a caterpillar (larva). The caterpillar takes three to four weeks to mature and reaches 4cm (1½in) in length. The newly hatched caterpillar is greenish yellow with a black head; as it matures, it develops black stripes with a pale outline and black dots along the body segments. In the mature form, it may live a further two weeks before becoming a pupa. Pupae are 1.5–2cm (½–1in) long and are contained in a spun cocoon; they may be surrounded by leaves bound together with white cobwebbing. The fully grown moth's wingspan is 4cm (1½in) and there are two forms. The commoner form has white wings and broad brown borders with white dots in the leading edge and the less common variety has entirely brown wings with white dots. Moths start to lay eggs within three days of emerging and they are mainly nocturnal. The life cycle of *C. perspectalis* is repeated three times a year, depending on conditions, and live forms can persist into October. Infection of box plants carries over into the following year on account of caterpillars remaining in the leaves, which can survive temperatures as low as −30°C. Caterpillars cease development and enter diapause when the length of daylight is less than 13.5h. The life cycle resumes with the emergence of caterpillars from diapause in March/April, depending on the temperature.

Identifying Attacks of Box Tree Caterpillar

Plants should be inspected every few days or at least once a week for signs of the caterpillar. On close inspection, damaged leaves may be apparent, some partly eaten, others brown. Skeletonized leaves are observed with only their ribs and outer margins intact and there is a characteristic presence of pale-coloured, wispy cobwebbing between leaves. Pale-green balls of frass (excrement) can be seen amongst the foliage.

Treatment of Box Tree Caterpillar – Hygiene

Once an attack by a caterpillar has been identified, plants should be searched for live insects and these should be removed and killed; a convenient method is to put them in a jar with washing-up detergent. Next, clear away the damaged parts of the plant with secateurs, and collect and burn the debris from the ground using a small hand-rake.

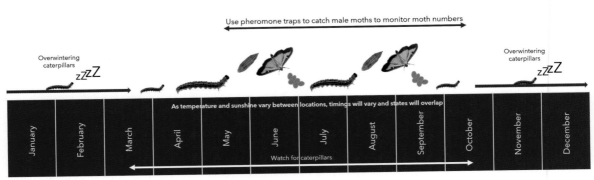

The life cycle of the box tree moth. Courtesy of the European Boxwood and Topiary Society.

Green pupa of *Cydalima perspectalis* with dark longitudinal stripes, indicating that it is at the beginning of pupation. It is nestled in box leaves with a silky cocoon.

Treatment of Box Tree Caterpillar – Pesticide Control

Biological agents are the first choice for treating attacks of box tree caterpillar. The most effective of the entomopathogenic agents is the bacterium *Bacillus thuringiensis*, available as Dipel (*B. thuringiensis* var. *kurstaki*) and Xen Tari (*B. thuringiensis* ssp. *aizawai*), which contain protein endotoxin crystals and living spores. Xen Tari is widely available, but in some countries, Dipel is restricted to use by holders of the appropriate licence. These compounds cause damage to the stomach and feeding stops within an hour; it should be applied at the first sign of infestation by caterpillars. As the bacteria proliferate, the insect is killed within one to three days. The spray should not be applied in wet conditions, although it remains effective once it has dried. These biological agents are inactive after approximately ten days as they are degraded by ultraviolet light. *Bacillus thuringiensis* has the advantage that it is safe to use and has no effect on beneficial garden insects.

Treatment of Box Tree Caterpillar – Other Pesticides

The use of insecticides has been prohibited or discouraged by regulatory authorities in recent years and the range of products available to the gardener is increasingly limited. This is because of the effect of these chemicals on beneficial insects and the adverse consequences for the ecology. If the gardener does choose to use insecticides to control box caterpillar, the relevant advice should be sought and a good source for this is the Royal Horticultural Society.

Pheromone Traps

Pheromone traps have a role in the identification and control of box moth infestation. The specific sex

The box tree moth has a wingspan of about 4cm (1½in) and has characteristic brown markings around the edges of the wings and a white dot on the leading edge. It is nocturnal and seldom sighted unless in a moth trap.

Damage due to box caterpillar with pale cobwebbing and brown and skeletonized leaves.

Damage due to box caterpillar with brown leaves, cobwebbing, damaged bark and frass balls. There is also healthy growth and this plant regenerated after spraying with an entomopathogenic agent and removal of damaged tissue.

pheromone for *C. perspectalis* is commercially available and is used in a trap for males of the species, which are attracted to the neck of the container where they flutter and fall in. Trapped moths are unavailable for reproduction, so the pheromone system has a small beneficial effect on control, but the entire male population of box moth preying on plants in a given area will not be significantly impacted. The traps are effective for a radius of 7–10m (23–33ft) and it may be necessary to place more than one in the garden. Pheromone traps are helpful in alerting the gardener to the presence of infestation by *C. perspectalis* before damage has been spotted and this should lead to extra vigilance in searching for the presence of caterpillars, so that measures to eradicate the pest can be carried out at the earliest time. An argument can be made for spraying plants approximately ten days after male moths have been trapped, even in the absence of observed caterpillars, in order to time treatment to the emergence of larvae from the eggs laid by the new generation of moths. Pheromone traps are, therefore, a very useful adjunct to the control of box moth caterpillar, but they are no substitute for regular inspection of plants for damage.

Pheromone Mating Disruptor

The same pheromone, z-11-hexadecenal, that is used in traps can be employed in seven times greater potency as a mating disruptor for the box moth. The idea is that the pheromone, when applied to box bushes, saturates the area with the smell that attracts male moths to their mate, so that they are no longer able to locate females.

A pheromone trap with a captive box moth. Pheromone traps are very useful as indicators of the activity of infestation with moths and should send an alert to search for signs of caterpillars.

The disruptor is applied as a gel from a cylinder under pressure produced by a foot pump and it needs to be administered twice in a season. At the time of writing, in late 2021, the product was available in several European countries with good results reported and trials are underway at Ham House in London (personal information, Chris Poole). This is an encouraging development and more information should be available about its release in the UK in due course.

Other Pests Affecting Box

Before the relatively recent arrival of box blight and box tree caterpillar there were pests and diseases that damaged box and had to be controlled, although none were as serious a threat as these. The most common of these is the psyllid, *Psylla buxi*.

Psyllid

The light-green nymph of *Psylla buxi* emerges early in the spring, usually April, and feeds on the new leaves, producing a white secretion that causes the leaves to become distorted and cupped, and taking the appearance of a miniature Brussels sprout. Slight infestation with psyllid is usually of low virulence and lasts for a limited time, so that the effects are usually not serious enough for control measures. There are a number of natural predators of *P. buxi*, including birds, ladybirds, wasps and ground beetles. However, significant infestation with psyllid is unattractive and serious infestations will affect growth, so that treatment with insecticides is warranted. Clipping may be helpful because the psyllid only affects the current, new growth of the stems; this will also impair the next year's growth because the damaged leaves do not grow for two years. There is one generation of psyllid a year. Active nymphs may be controlled with insecticidal oil/soaps or a residual foliar-absorbed pesticide.

Scale

There are a number of scale insects that attack box and in the UK, *Lepidosaphes ulmi* (mussel scale) is occa-

New leaves affected by psyllid, with characteristic cupping deformity.

sionally seen. Mussel scale is a sap-sucking insect, 3mm (⅒in) long that is concealed under scales; it has the appearance of the shellfish of the same name. This scale insect generally hides on two- to four-year-old stems, inside the shrub, and is not often detected without careful inspection. Heavy infestations have a deleterious effect on growth. The most effective time to take action with an insecticide is in late May and June.

Box Leafmining Gall Midge

In some parts of the world, including the USA, this is a serious insect pest of box. Partly grown larvae winter within the leaf and emerge in the spring, developing into yellow-orange pupae, which morph into flies, approximately 1cm (⅖in) in length, resembling orange mosquitos. Damage is caused by the larvae feeding on leaves, which cause oval discolouration and swelling on the underneath. In severe infestations, which rarely occur in the UK, shedding of leaves can be extensive. Once the flies have emerged, skins of pupae (mines) can be seen hanging down from the underside of the leaf. Control is necessary only if the plant is heavily infested. In this case, consider applying an insecticide when the new leaves are fully formed in May, with one additional application six to eight weeks later.

Mites

The spider mite that affects box is fairly widespread and in hot, dry sites the damage can be severe. When the attack by the mite is extensive, the plant takes on a silvery appearance. However, the damage may be inconspicuous because it is hidden by dense, new leaves and affects second- and third-year growth. The mite itself is very inconspicuous and it causes damage to leaves by sucking out the sap of epidermal cells, leaving a fine, pale stippling, due to the absence of chlorophyll. This results in a dysfunctional leaf, unable to produce carbohydrates through photosynthesis and very slowly, through several years, the box produces fewer and smaller leaves. This leads to a general decline and the shrub usually fails as a result of additional climatic stress. The best way to assess the level of infestation with mite is to bang a branch over a piece of card and count the number of spiders that fall out: twenty-five or more is considered to be a significant enough problem to use control measures. The best agent to use to reduce numbers is a spray based on fatty acids or plant oils (horticultural oil). A number of applications need to be made at five-day intervals.

INDEX